Intervention Strategies for Sexual Abuse

Robert H. Rencken

D1023915

Copyright © 1989 by the American Association for Counseling and Development

All rights reserved.

American Association for Counseling and Development
5999 Stevenson Avenue
Alexandria, VA 22304

Cover design by Sarah Jane Valdez

Library of Congress Cataloging-in-Publication Data

Rencken, Robert H.
    Intervention strategies for sexual abuse.

    Includes index.
    1. Child molesting—Treatment. 2. Sexually abused children.
    3. Adult child sexual abuse victims. I. Title.
    RC560.C46R46   1989   616.85'83   89-6895
    ISBN 1-055620-057-9

Printed in the United States of America.

To my children, their children, and our children

CONTENTS

Introduction ix

Chapter 1: Overview 1

The Problem 1
Approaching the Problem 12
Dynamics 16
Legal Issues and the Criminal Justice System 22

Chapter 2: Intervention Strategies—Victim 29

The Young Child 30
The Middle Child 39
The Adolescent 61

Chapter 3: Intervention Strategies—Offender 83

Assessment/Evaluation 85
Diagnosis, Categorization, and Treatment Planning 91
Treatment 99

**Chapter 4: Intervention Strategies—The Family and
Adult Survivors** 111

Intervention Strategies—The Family 111
Interventions—Adult Survivors 119

Chapter 5: Case Studies 127

A—Dictatorial/Possessive Father 127
B—Dependent Father 136
C—Pseudoadult Child 143
D—Pedophile 147
E—Pedophile 150
F—Adolescent Survivor 151
G—Adult Survivor 154

H—Female Offender 157
I—Isolated Treatment of Victim 161

Chapter 6: The Road Ahead 165

Prevention and Education 165
The Challenge 168

Glossary 171
Resources 175
References 177
Index 181

ACKNOWLEDGMENTS

I wish to gratefully acknowledge the direct and indirect contributions of many people. I particularly single out:

Sara Welchert, for her patient and diligent typing;

Lizbeth Gray, Jacqueline Saltz, and my colleague and co-therapist, Jean Wortman, for their feedback on the manuscript;

The AACD publications staff and Media Committee for their encouragement and professionalism;

My colleagues at El Dorado Psychological Associates, Sunnyside Unified School District, and Las Familias Treatment Program; and my national family, the American Mental Health Counselors Association;

My clients, from whom I have learned courage, persistence, and love;

And, most of all, my lover and partner, Kay, whose patience, acceptance, and nurturance of children is exceeded only by the same qualities directed at me.

INTRODUCTION

In traveling around the country doing workshops and seminars on the issues of sexual abuse, incest, and childhood sexuality, I have been consistently impressed with the range and diversity of professionals and other caregivers who are hungry for information. These are not people who want to specialize in the treatment of sexual abuse. In fact, many of them wish that it had never reared its head in their professional or personal life and wish that it would simply go away.

The information for which they hunger is basic and immediate—How should a known victim be treated in school? Why do "those perverts" do it? How does a history of abuse affect a college student's relationships? What strategies can be effective in intervening in a sexual abuse situation even if I am not the primary counselor or therapist?

Although many fine resource books have been recently published in the field of sexual abuse, many are geared toward the specialized treatment of one segment of the population affected (healing the survivor, behavioral treatment of the offender, play therapy with the young victim) or may add to the confusion of the consumer or clinician through unclear jargon and nonstandard categorization (e.g., pedophilia, molest, incest, deviant behavior, rape, sexaholism). For the average counselor or human development professional in the field, it might seem necessary to read a dozen books and attend two or three workshops to gain a basic understanding of the problem and to learn intervention strategies.

The intent of this book is to provide a clear and basic framework for understanding the dimensions (scope, taxonomy, philosophy) and dynamics (individual, familial, societal) of pedosexual behavior, particularly child sexual abuse. The major focus will be on the implementation of integrated intervention strategies for any professional who faces only one "piece of the puzzle."

Sexual abuse is a complex problem that is extremely taxing and challenging for the counselor/psychotherapist. The ideal counselor should be skilled in individual adult counseling, play therapy, marriage/relationship work, group process with children and adults, behavior modification, sex therapy, the criminal justice system, and family systems, among other areas. Many of us feel more comfortable and competent in some of these areas than in others. It is essential that we recognize this and focus our interventions within our area of competence and expertise. This book will provide strategies for those interventions as well as a sense of the "big picture" that puts those interventions into an integrated perspective.

It will be tempting for the reader to flip directly to strategies applicable to his or her situation or population; for the school counselor to go to the "victim" section or the college dean to go to the "survivor" section. I believe, however, that this would deny the larger perspective and reinforce one of the problems we currently have—counselors working at cross-purposes and, sometimes, even adversarially. I do encourage *rereading* sections of particular interest. I also strongly encourage all professionals to ask themselves how they can be a part of the prevention of this major problem through treatment, advocacy, and research.

The treatment of individuals and families involved in sexual abuse has been the most rewarding part of my professional career. I hope that I can share some of that enthusiasm, encouragement, and empowerment.

CHAPTER 1

OVERVIEW

The Problem

It would be nice if somebody else had the problem. Not exactly "nice," but we could have the safety and luxury of sitting back and feeling sorry for "that poor kid." Maybe life was a little simpler before I knew very much about sexual abuse.

Counselors in all settings are, however, dealing with sexual abuse. Like it or not, prepared or not, counselors are hearing "the words" from many sources. We hear the 9-year-old tell about his neighbor forcing fellatio on him. We hear the 16-year-old tell about long-term coitus with her stepfather. We hear of the college student worrying about relationships because of her secret of abuse as a child. We hear the 30-year-old divorced woman tell of her generalized anger toward men. We hear about the tragic rape and murder of a 10-year-old boy. We hear, and hear about, the horror stories of sexual abuse.

When I ask counselors how they react to sexual abuse, some common feelings surface: disgust, anger, sympathy, pity, rage. Many counselors also feel an accompanying sense of helplessness. What can I do to alleviate this devastating problem? Can I be more than an emotional Band-Aid? How can I find the time to deal with something this big? How can I erase what has happened? How can I deal with my own feelings and reactions?

The feelings and the questions make sense. Most counselors, psychotherapists, social workers, psychologists, psychiatrists, and

1

other helping professionals have had little or no academic training about sexual abuse. Some have sought out workshops, seminars, or books that have possibly even added to the feeling of being overwhelmed. The intention of this volume is to unravel some of the complexity of the dynamics and treatment of sexual abuse so that you can make meaningful interventions in the lives of your clients, whether as a primary or supportive therapist. Although this book is not intended to train you as an expert or specialist in the field, it may be a helpful foundation and resource tool.

• • •

Can you visualize a snow-covered volcano? That's a fair metaphor for sexual abuse in several ways:

- Most of the time, to the casual observer, things not only look normal but better than normal.
- Even when the volcano is dormant, the snow hides treacherous rocks and holes. The secret of sexual abuse covers up both the behavior and damage and may "successfully" cover them for years before the unsuspecting victim/survivor trips and falls.
- The eruption of the volcano symbolizes the tremendous potential force of the anger and rage of the victim.
- The mixing of lava and snow is typical of the many dilemmas involved—love/hate, fear/guilt, power/weakness.
- After the eruption, the lava also leaves scars, a new face on the mountain. Of course, this new face, like the old one, can be covered with snow. Again, on the surface, the scars may not be visible and look "normal."
- Then there are other family members, friends, and society who are also buried in lava and snow as indirect victims.
- Finally, of course, the potential for further eruption continues, unpredictable in time, intensity, and cause. We see the anger, rage, and pain years after abuse has ceased.

We will be returning to this metaphor. For now, suffice it to say that the issues of sexual abuse are among the most complicated and elusive that we as counselors and therapists face. As often as not, it seems that things are not what they seem because of denials, rationalizations, secrets, repression, fear, ambivalence, surface normality, and societal bias.

What do we know for sure? Not much. Although the interest in sexual abuse has certainly increased dramatically in the last several years, there has been little research besides clinical practice itself. We have done a surprisingly good job, in fact, of dealing with these issues through clinical networking rather than experimental, or even descriptive, research. Much, if not most, of the research in this book is attributable to the clinical experience of dozens of therapists whose information is shared verbally as well as literally.

Research in this area faces major obstacles: lack of data (sketchy data available only on reported cases), greatly varying terminology in both legal and scientific circles (e.g., fondling, intercourse, and pederasty each has varying definitions), differing legal statutes and punishments, the primary need to protect child victims, and strong societal biases.

What we do know about sexual abuse in terms of statistics is summarized effectively in Finkelhor's (1984) research:

- Incidence research shows that between 8% to 38% of women and 5% to 9% of men in the United States have been victimized.
- Sexual abuse is an international concern, although specific statistics are not available.
- Sexual abuse is committed primarily by men (Finkelhor, 1979; Bell & Weinberg, 1978). Among victims, 95% of women and 80% of men are abused by men.
- Sexual abuse essentially, by definition, is harmful.
- The most common ages of victims are 8 through 12, with many cases outside of that span.
- Stepfathers may be five times as likely to victimize a daughter sexually than fathers are, although other family members (brothers, uncles, grandfathers) could be offenders.
- Most female victimization occurs within the family.
- Boys are more likely to be abused outside the family than are girls.

This information is of help, but even these facts may change. We think that despite media attention on the subject, particularly on the issue of false allegations (Spiegel, 1988), we continue to see underreporting because of the following observations:

- Despite Finkelhor's (1984) attempts at gaining data from parent reports, most data are gathered from retrospective reports of previously unreported incidents.
- Increasingly severe penalties for offenders may be discouraging children from reporting or testifying against a family

member. Data to support this contention are particularly difficult to obtain and interpret.

- Adults are so uncomfortable with both sexual and sexual abuse issues that they may have a tendency "not to get involved" in reporting.
- The victimization of boys is minimized because of our societal sexist beliefs that only girls are victims, only men are offenders, and boys can't cry (or tattle or feel or care) and should not only "take it" but, somehow, actually enjoy it.
- Children are afraid to report.
- Abuse is masked by other behavior (running away, substance abuse, suicide, shyness, withdrawal).
- Children are not believed.

Regardless of the exact statistics, and even when using conservative estimates, there are hundreds of thousands of cases of sexual abuse each year. Clearly, we are a society that abuses, exploits, and victimizes those that are less powerful—the children.

Impact

Measuring the impact of sexual abuse on children entails the same kind of obstacles as does incidence research. We can easily talk about the trauma of abuse, yet we know that children's reactions are not predictable or universal. We can talk about future difficulties with healthy sexual functioning and self-esteem (Herman, 1981), but we cannot predict how or when those effects may materialize.

We can make some general statements about effects or potential effects which, although clearly not universal, are helpful for us in treating and supporting families, victims, and survivors of sexual abuse.

1. The process of sexualization, discussed in chapter 2 on intervention strategies for the victim, is defined as an anomaly that affects the child's general adjustment by causing the child to skip stages of psychological development as a result of a sexual experience.
2. The child loses trust, security, and, as a result, the essence of childhood.
3. The child experiences ambivalent feelings—love and hate, rage and guilt, stoicism and fear—that are difficult even for adults.

4. The message is loud and clear that sex is exploitive, demanding, hurtful (and painful), and interwoven with power and manipulation, reinforcing our societal sex negativity and setting up the cycle of abuse.
5. Defenses are created that, although initially functional, become obstacles to treatment and successful adjustment: denial, repression, dissociation, anorgasmia, anorexia, obesity, substance use/abuse, running away; and, the ultimate result:
6. Death, by overt or covert suicide, or homicide.

The impact of sexual abuse is felt not only by the victim, as difficult as that may be. The rest of the family, peers, and society are affected as well. Yet, the one person who is not often considered when we discuss impact is the offender. The most obvious consequences for sexual abuse are criminal prosecution or removal from the home. Issues of the criminal justice system will be expanded in a later section, but clearly the threat of arrest, prison, probation, or mandated separation from the victim or the offender's family presents emotional, relational, financial, and employment problems. This is not to discount the offender's responsibility or to imply that the offender doesn't "deserve" the consequences. Rather, it is necessary to acknowledge the pain, guilt (often at suicidal intensity), and confusion that *most* sexual abusers feel (although there are certainly exceptions). This pain may be present both before and after the report and, if untreated, continue indefinitely.

Probably the most persistent conflict on a day-to-day basis is experienced by the nonoffending spouse in intrafamilial abuse. The strained and dysfunctional marital relationship is often both the cause and effect of abuse. The mother is torn between loyalty toward/support of/dependency on her husband on one side, and protection and support of her child on the other. Unfortunately, this conflict is too often resolved through denial, divorce, or physical or psychological abandonment.

Siblings may also be victims, for they are not only fearful of being abused themselves but also may have been aware of the abuse and be unwitting keepers of the family "secret." They may defend against this fear and guilt by blaming the victim of abuse. If they can rationalize that the victim "asked for it" or "enjoyed it," then they can be less conflicted about loving the father.

Peers also may be affected and be torn between supporting and blaming the victim. The friend, in fact, may be involved in the report. Frequently the victim will admit the abuse to a friend, who tells her or his parent, who in turn reports to authorities. The most effective therapy group, not surprisingly, is the peer victim/survivor group.

The damage of sexual abuse to society is seen in several systems. Obviously, the damage to the family as the foundation of society affects basic affectional and relational systems. Sexualization affects societal concerns such as early pregnancy and sexually transmitted diseases. Economic costs include direct costs (protection, prosecution, punishment) and indirect costs (loss of productivity, welfare support, underemployment).

Finally, we need to look at the impact of sexual abuse on the counseling profession and the practice of psychotherapy, regardless of professional affiliation. It was not too long ago that we, as counselors and therapists, were ignoring or actively denying the problem. We then, by my observation, seemed to move to a stage of buck-passing where we became more aware of the problem, reported as we were required, but still wanted "others" to take care of it (Child Protective Services, law enforcement, mental health system). Now, I think, we are making the transition to a more directly active role: probing for the possibility of abuse in child and adult clients, providing primary therapy for victims, offenders, and families, or taking an important supportive role with treatment teams and coordinating with various agencies. Counselors in all settings are on the "front line" in confronting this issue, *like it or not*! We have an ethical responsibility to be prepared.

Taxonomy

One of the biggest obstacles in research, education, and treatment of sexual abuse is the lack of common terminology and taxonomy (Waterman & Lusk, 1986). In fact, this is a significant problem in sexological research and writing in general (M. Diamond, personal communication, 1987). Understanding of the issues is confounded by philosophical differences (sexual behavior vs. abuse), ill-defined concepts (sexual abuse, incest, molestation), changing definitions, legal inconsistencies (intercourse, consensuality), and prejudicial labels (molester, pervert, promiscuous, deviate, babyraper). The reader is referred to the Glossary for clarification of terms, with the caveat that again, there is no standard for terminology, and these definitions may vary from one researcher or clinician to another.

I have been using the term *pedosexual* as a generic term for any sexual contact involving a child or adolescent. Although this is stretching the typical usage of the prefix, *pedo-*, to include adolescents, it is helpful because of the overlapping of behaviors. The term is reasonably objective and inclusive and provides us with the opportunity to classify behavior, dynamics, participants, and setting. It should be used as an adjective (pedosexual behavior), rather than as a noun ("he is a pedosexual").

Attempts at taxonomy in this field have included bipolar classifications such as Groth and Birnbaum's (1978) fixated versus regressed offender or Giaretto's (1982) focus on intrafamilial versus extrafamilial abuse, or Finkelhor's (1984) four preconditions. All of these dimensions need to be included in a taxonomy.

The pedosexual taxonomy has three axes: age of participants, setting (intra- vs. extrafamilial), and five categories of offender dynamics. This type of highly specific taxonomy will result in more specific clinical and descriptive research and improved clinical communication.

In using the taxonomy, we can abbreviate these axes:

- The five possible age combinations become C/C (child-child), C/Ado (child-adolescent), C/Adu (child-adult), Ado/Ado (adolescent-adolescent), and Ado-Adu (adolescent-adult).
- The setting is either E (extrafamilial) or I (intrafamilial).
- The offender dynamics become R (regressed), Ra (rapist), P (pedophile), A (addictive/compulsive), or S (symptomatic).

Thus, for example, "C/Adu,I,R" indicates intrafamilial pedosexual contact between a regressed adult and a prepubertal child.

It is also essential to describe behavior clearly and specifically. Instead of "fondling," we need to specify whether or not there is digital penetration or clitoral stimulation, and whether the behavior is active or receptive. Similarly, instead of "oral sex," we need to specify fellatio or cunnilingus, and instead of "intercourse," specify penile-vaginal, penile-femoral, and so forth. Specifying the behavior, of course, requires the correct use of basic anatomical terms. One of the most common errors is to refer to the "vagina" when meaning "labia."

The first axis the counselor needs to identify is setting, that is, whether the pedosexual behavior took place within or outside the family unit. "Intrafamilial" uses the "living unit" as a frame of reference. It includes those family members living together regardless of blood or legal relationship, including "live-in boyfriends" and, of course, stepparents. It does not typically include extended family unless they are living together or are emotionally close.

The age of the participants can be categorized by a matrix of child (prepubertal), adolescent (pubescent to 18 years old), and adult, yielding six possible combinations: child-child, child-adolescent, child-adult, adolescent-adolescent, adolescent-adult, and adult-adult. Because our focus is on pedosexual contact, we will not discuss the adult-adult combination even though sexual abuse does occur between adults and can be a criminal offense. The five remaining combinations are important in the taxonomy because they help to describe potential power imbalances.

Child-child. The frequency of child-child sexual contact has not been researched. Although we have probably classified most cases as "sex play," (e.g., "playing doctor"), this generalization may be less helpful than in the past. Because we have typically described abuse (either physical or sexual) in terms of a power differential, a 5-year age difference has frequently been adopted as significant for that power difference (Finkelhor, 1984). We are more often, however, seeing situations that involve clearly coercive (and probably abusive) behaviors involving children with little or no age difference. This seems to occur when one child has been powerfully sexualized. The assumption that either all child-child contacts are innocent or all are harmful is an oversimplification. The key factors in assessing actual or potential damage involve determining developmental appropriateness (Yates, 1978) and coercion (Finkelhor, 1984) regardless of age difference.

Adolescent-adolescent. Like child-child contacts, we are not typically concerned about abusive issues in this situation unless, again, we are confronted with a power differential. The 5-year age difference provides a helpful guideline but is even further complicated by size differential between sexes as well as consensus issues. Age of consensus is a significant societal quandary that will not be settled here. Again, the extent of coercion is critical whether we label a behavior as abusive, exploitive, or "date-rape."

Child-adolescent. The issue of power differential is much clearer in this combination although coercion may be more implicit, based on physical and cognitive differences. This area needs considerable research because the dynamics or motivation of an adolescent "offender" may be very different than those of an adult offender.

Adolescent-adult. Although popular opinion would have us believe that most molestful behavior happens in this age group, it seems clear that most contact is initiated at a younger age and may continue into this range (Finkelhor, 1984).

Child-adult. The power differential, of course, is clearest here. Legally and psychologically, this age combination is most likely to be described as abusive.

Dynamics

The third dimension of the pedosexual taxonomy is based on the dynamics of the offender. Clearly this is the most subjective component and the one that will be most susceptible to change with continuing research. It is necessary, however, to proceed with the taxonomy for scientific, clinical, and political purposes. (The latter become apparent when we see legislation enacted based on misinformation and miscategorization.) The following proposed categories are *not* completely discrete.

Regressed. The regressed (as opposed to fixated) offender was identified by Groth and Birnbaum (1978) as one who has apparently not exhibited any predominant sexual attraction to significantly younger persons during his sexual development. Although this category has been associated with intrafamilial abuse, it is also typical of the dynamics in much extrafamilial pedosexual contact. The exact etiology of the regression may differ: power issues, severe stress, substance abuse, marital dysfunction, history of physical or sexual abuse, or a combination. Sexual arousal patterns vary, with some cases seeming to entail no erection or other arousal whereas others include complex sexual fantasy through to orgasm. The presence of sexual arousal does *not* necessarily indicate a paraphilia, or deviance from the norm, unless it is a predominant pattern of arousal by, attraction to, or preference for children. This category produces the largest number of offenders.

Pedophile. The definition of pedophilia (one of the paraphilias) has changed somewhat from the DSM-III to the DSM-IIIR, the American Psychiatric Association's (1987) *Diagnostic and Statistical Manual of Mental Disorders, Third Edition, Revised.* The major criteron, however, is still clearly a consistent and preferred sexual attraction to prepubertal children. In this taxonomy, the related paraphilias are included: hebephilia (adolescent girls) and ephebophilia (adolescent boys), although the dynamics of these latter two may be closer to those of adult attraction. Pedophilia is linked with Groth and Birnbaum's (1978) category of the fixated offender (sexually attracted primarily or exclusively to significantly younger persons). There are some pedophiles, however, who do give at least surface indications of mature development but have retained the primary attraction to children. Although pedophiles may be a statistical minority, each is likely to affect multiple victims, sometimes numbering into the hundreds.

Addicted/compulsive. Much recent attention has been given to the concept of the sex addict (or sexaholic or sexually compulsive person) (Carnes, 1983). Although research still has not clarified this phenomenon generally, certainly as it relates to pedosexual contact, there is much interest in the relationship between compulsive sexual behavior (variously defined and interpreted) and other addictive/compulsive disorders. It seems that pedosexual behavior may be one of the behaviors that appear in a cluster along with other behaviors (usually one to three) including compulsive masturbation, voyeurism, exhibitionism, or dependence on prostitution or on sexually explicit media. Children, probably young adolescent girls, may become "targets of opportunity" for the sexually compulsive individual. In other words, children may be more easily available than more typical adult partners. Although other pedosexual behavior patterns also may have compulsive or dependent elements, this pattern is converse; that is, the compulsion is primary and the child contact incidental.

Rapist. The primary pattern of the rapist is the use of sexual behavior as an expression of violence. Specific dynamics may include those of power, anger, or sadism, as described by Groth (1979). Precise legal and scientific criteria for defining rape may differ. The definition of "forcible penetration or attempted penetration" will be used in this book. The latter is included because the offender's intent and the victim's trauma are essentially the same whether or not penetration is actually achieved. Although pedosexual rape is relatively infrequent compared to either adult rape or other pedosexual contact, it understandably commands much public attention. Child rape tragically also may result in homicide or severe physical trauma, precipitating legislative or prosecutorial redress against all "child molesters." The issue of sexual arousal, particularly in the child rapist, is vague. The rapist tends to repeat his behavior with a high rate of recidivism, even if he has been convicted and incarcerated.

Symptomatic. This category of the taxonomy describes offenders whose pedosexual behavior is symptomatic of some other primary disorder. Examples of such primary disorders include schizophrenia, mental retardation, substance abuse or dependence (use of alcohol as a disinhibitor would not make it a primary disorder), or major depression. We should exercise caution that we do not attribute causation; that is, schizophrenia does not *cause* the pedosexual contact but that contact may be one symptom of schizophrenia. It can also be noted that many offenders become depressed, anxious, or distressed *after* the pedosexual contact or report but, again, such depression or distress would not be considered a primary disorder for our purposes. Although this category may have the smallest number of offenders, it bears clinical attention because the primary disorder is sometimes overlooked in treatment or incarceration/probation decisions.

Use of This Taxonomy

Although the taxonomy described in this section of chapter 1 would provide a helpful framework for research, the initial focus needs to be on clinical issues. As noted, the DSM system addresses only one aspect of the problem of sexual abuse—pedophilia. Those affected by pedosexual contact, victim or offender, may well have one of a variety of diagnoses on the DSM Axis I (mental disorder) or II (personality disorder), but these do not adequately relate to sexual abuse. Like the DSM, this taxonomy should be helpful for more precise clinical communication with a minimum of judgmental terminology.

All three dimensions of pedosexual taxonomy (setting, age group, and dynamics) should be used in describing child-adolescent, child-adult, and adolescent-adult contacts. When known, the duration or frequency of the behavior should also be noted (e.g., "one-time digital-anal penetration" or "weekly penile-vaginal coitus for 6 months").

This taxonomy will be used in discussions of dynamics and interventions in the rest of the book.

Approaching the Problem

One of the most important tasks of any counselor is to clearly identify philosophical assumptions, personal values, and societal/ environmental atmosphere surrounding any treatment situation. This is particularly true in working with sexual abuse. Counselors in the general area of sexuality have long been aware of the need for self-awareness regarding their own attitudes, values, and beliefs as well as sensitivity to others' values, belief systems, and decision-making processes. When the focus narrows to sex offenses, the need for sensitivity and awareness increases. In turn, when the focus narrows further to child sexual abuse, the counselor needs to be acutely aware of his or her assumptions, values, and societal/ environmental atmosphere. This section will examine some of these areas.

Most professionals who specialize in dealing with pedosexual issues have been asked, "How can you handle those perversions? Why do you deal with those slimeballs? How can you stand being in the same room with them? Why don't they just cut their balls off?" It is not unusual for people actually to question or impugn the motivation, ethics, or integrity of those working with the offender population or, indeed, with sexual abuse in general. Some critics will praise therapists working with children/victims/survivors but vilify those working with offenders. This kind of criticism is certainly difficult for the counselor to hear and reinforces the need to examine the personal agenda closely.

Societal prejudice against "molesters" has not been specifically investigated but may be based on:

1. outrage against the victimization of children;
2. general negativity about sex;
3. lack of knowledge about different forms of pedosexual contact including issues of arousal, behavior, and treatability;
4. images of the raincoat-clad "dirty old man";
5. association with other negative issues (valid or not) such as pornography and alcoholism;
6. assumptions of male sexual inadequacy; that is, offenders aren't good enough for "real sex"; and
7. fear that "it could happen to me."

Societal prejudice could be tolerated were it not for the impact on the children and their families. Children's natural egocentricity leads them to conclude that they are the ones who created the abuse situation by being "bad." The more negative society is, the more the child feels it. It is typical for the child to blame her- or himself for all the disruption in the family a report causes.

In talking with adult survivors of different forms of pedosexual contact, it becomes clear that they kept "the secret" for years not only to protect the offender and the rest of the family, but also out of fear of being seen as tainted or culpable. The feelings of shame and, sometimes blame, that rape victims report are magnified by the distortions of normal child reactions. In the victim's mind, ambivalence and confusion may be more immediate than the rage and fear that we may expect. Societal prejudice frequently complicates this ambivalence and prevents the victim from moving on.

So, if societal prejudice can have such negative results, should we turn around and defend pedosexual behavior? *Absolutely not!* Sexual abuse clearly remains a problem of major proportions, and the offenders must be held both accountable and totally responsible for their behavior. How can a counselor demand that accountability without condemning the offender? How can the counselor treat the victim without pity? How can the counselor maintain any sense of optimism? I believe that a set of philosophical assumptions may be necessary before we pursue issues of dynamics and treatment.

The Problem Is Treatable

Although some pedosexual offenders (pedophiles and addicts) may be very resistant to treatment, the majority of clients with whom counselors will work can and will improve dramatically with treatment. This applies to victims, survivors, families, as well as offenders. Indeed, despite some of the negative issues described earlier, many therapists see their work with abusive families as extremely rewarding because of the changes that individuals and families show during treatment. This is particularly true when family units are able to proceed through the treatment process together.

Giaretto's (1982) reports of the low recidivism of offenders in his model family treatment program are corroborated by our experience; we have documented only six reported cases of repeated molestation in 8 years in approximately 200 cases. In fact, using Giaretto's criteria of a minimum of 10 sessions and successful termination, the number of families who experienced recidivism is reduced to two. Furthermore, anecdotal reports from families indicate that couples who do not divorce are not only functioning better than at the time of abuse, but probably better than most families function. Of course, many couples do choose divorce, both early in the process and during treatment. After a divorce, many spouses and families drop out of treatment, but others choose to continue in treatment and benefit remarkably.

The Child Is the Primary Client

The assumption that the child (victim) is the primary client is valid whether the counselor is treating the child directly, treating the offender, or any of the family. It is true even if the counselor never sees the child, or acts as a consultant for the defense. Keeping the child (victim) and children (potential victims) as the primary focus is an ongoing issue, with the question, "What is best for the child?", as the "bottom line." Answers to that question, of course, are neither easy nor unanimous. The question pervades reporting, investigating, treatment plans, visitation, and, eventually, decisions regarding reunification or treatment termination of the victim or offender.

Assuming that the child is the primary client enables resolving the ethical dilemma of "Who is my client?" It places the counselor/therapist in a very different role from that of others in the adversarial system. It does not, however, prevent appropriate advocacy for the adult client (offender or spouse) either within the legal or mental health system. In fact, such advocacy may well result in significant benefit to the child.

Treatment Is Prevention

It could be said that sexual abuse treatment is, by definition, post facto, after the abuse and report have occurred. Sometimes months or years may have passed since the last incident. Treatment cannot erase what already has happened. It can, however, prevent reoccurrence for both the victim and, by treating the offender, for future victims. By treating the victim, future abuse also may be prevented because many victims later become offenders. Treatment also acts as prevention for other problems, again, for both victim and offender. The primary focus of treatment, then, is as much prevention as rehabilitation. Likewise, the focus of the criminal justice system could well be treatment and prevention as well as punishment.

The Offender Is 100% Responsible for the Abuse

This assumption will be discussed in some detail in the treatment sections of the book. It is a basic assumption in dealing with any part of the sexual abuse problem and is possibly the single most important factor for the offender to accept. There are two facets to this assumption: one is that *no one* else can be responsible for the choice made by the offender (neither the "seductive" child nor the "nagging" spouse); second, *nothing* else can be blamed (alcohol, finances, abuse history, the libido). Even if a sophisticated rationale or etiology is discovered, the offender *always* bears the responsibility for making the choice to cross the line into pedosexual contact. The responsibility issue, therefore, is not one of blame, judgment, or guilt, but rather a positive focus that initiates the change process.

The Offender Is Accountable to Society

Not only is the offender responsible for the behavior and accountable to the victim and family, but also to society at large. Because sexual abuse/contact/assault/molestation are violations of the law, the offender may face prosecution, sentencing, probation, or incarceration depending on variables that the counselor typically cannot control. This is an unusual dimension for many counselors and affects such standard practices as voluntary treatment and privileged communication. To some extent, the counselor also becomes accountable to society.

Integrated Team Treatment

The nature of sexual abuse is complex and almost always involves multiple counselors/therapists. Coordinated assessment and treatment planning may involve not only therapists but also Child Protective Services, probation departments, law enforcement, medical staff, school personnel, and others. The counselor, whether acting in a primary or supportive role, will need to be able to effectively communicate with, and support, the team while maintaining an appropriate advocacy and protection posture.

Unconditional Positive Regard

This most basic counseling assumption may well be significantly tested. Feelings of anger, frustration, disgust, pity, or contempt can obviously color the objectivity and regard for the client (offender). It is essential for the counselor to make a self-assessment, with unconditional positive regard as an important criterion. It may be better to withdraw from a case rather than to lose this focus.

Sex Positivism

It is essential for the counselor to maintain a positive attitude regarding sexuality. Specifically, sexuality is best regarded as a positive force for the individual and society even if it is sometimes used in negative ways.

I believe these assumptions not only allow, but demand, a positive approach to clients and to the problems of pedosexual contact and, particularly, abuse. This positive approach can be effective, if not perfect, regardless of a particular pathology or dysfunction.

Dynamics

The most consistent question is, "Why does sexual abuse occur?"

The most consistent answer is, "I don't know."

The question comes from victims, spouses, family, friends, judges, Child Protective Services, legislators, and, yes, offenders.

The answer comes from victims, spouses, researchers, counselors, authors, and, yes, offenders.

You may be frustrated. You were hoping to get the answer to the "why" question by reading this book. Why isn't there a simple answer?

We'd all like a relatively simple answer to the question, hoping that researchers can identify a missing gene, a mutant virus, or a hormone imbalance. Barring such a physiological breakthrough, we would like a simple psychosocial explanation—history of abuse, lack of oral gratification, contingency reinforcement—but the problem is too complex and the variables too heterogeneous. As reflected in the taxonomy, there are hundreds of possible combinations of behaviors, participants, settings, and dynamics.

Perhaps we may even be asking the wrong question. Rather than looking for the "why," which implies causation, we need to look at the "how." How was the abuse set up? How did disinhibiting factors work? How was the secret kept? How can we protect the child?

"How did this happen?" becomes a question of description rather than causation, and therefore infinitely easier to handle. It may also be equally effective in the treatment process because it leads to the end goal, "How can we make sure it doesn't happen again?"

Knowledge of individual, familial, and societal dynamics, both general and case-specific, leads to a much clearer picture of past, present, and future functioning.

A metaphor that I typically use with clients is to picture their abuse situation as a jigsaw puzzle without the box cover, total confusion without a sense of what the puzzle is going to look like when completed. At first, there is a sense of despair—the task seems overwhelming and a lot of hard work is spent in sorting out pieces and colors with no matches. The counselor hasn't seen this puzzle either but has seen other puzzles like it (understands dynamics) and knows some ways of dealing with them by finding straight edges and like colors (intervention strategies). With those strategies, a match is found, then another, and another. There is a glimmer of encouragement as matches lead to patterns, which accelerates the process. Sometimes the counselor makes a match or points one out but, mostly, the client has to see the matches. Finally, the picture emerges. Most of the time, this happens even if *all* the pieces don't fit and are in place. The puzzle does not have to be 100% perfect!

Clearly, understanding dynamics can help with seeing *how* things fit. (Did you ever try to figure out the *why* of a jigsaw puzzle?) We will look at dynamics, beginning at the societal level, to give us some clues.

Societal Dynamics

It is difficult for many of us to look at societal issues because they imply some responsibility on our part for the existence of the problem of sexual abuse. And, how does this fit with the philosophical assumption that the offender is 100% responsible for the abuse?

Society and its microcosm, the family, both create the environment for abuse, just as they create the environment for healthy functioning, growth, and development. Issues at the societal level may be pervasive and, at the same time, subtle and resistant to change. The following are some issues to consider.

1. We remain a male-controlled society. It is no coincidence that pedosexual contact (especially pedophilia and rape) is essentially a male phenomenon (Finkelhor, 1984). Although the number of female offenders may be underreported for a number of reasons, men clearly predominate (so much so that masculine pronouns are used in this book to refer to offenders). As long as a control/power imbalance exists, women and children risk being seen as available for, submissive to, dependent on, or, at the extreme, chattel of men. Under these conditions, even at their most benign form, the man can feel a sense of permission to engage in sexual behavior. These are, of course, the same conditions that contribute to spouse rape, battering, physical child abuse, neglect, and lack of support.

2. Despite the surface value we place on precocity and pseudoadult behavior, children are at the lowest point of the control/power ladder. Their lack of power (physical, verbal, role) increases the chance of exploitation, manipulation, and abuse. Despite media attention to these issues, we continue to be a society that devalues children and *does not believe* them. Also, with some intention, we keep children powerless in the sexual arena by not providing enough information on sexuality in general and abuse prevention in particular.

3. We also remain a sex-negative society (Rencken, 1986). We acknowledge sexuality as positive in the context of reproduction and marriage but label other expressions of sexuality as negative to one extent or another. Sex is used exploitively to sell products, people, and programs. Sex becomes a powerful tool and weapon rather than an expression of intimacy.

4. We are a society that believes in punishment as problem resolution. We think longer prison sentences (or execution or castration) will reduce crime. We think that nations that offend us should be "nuked." We think children should be physically punished at school (Maurer, 1972–1988) and at home (Dobson, 1970). We believe that might makes right.

Family Dynamics

There is little empirical research on family style; that is, how the abusive family unit functions. There are indications that sexual abuse families tend to be isolative, rigid, and conservative/traditional in style (Finkelhor, 1979; Herman, 1981). They tend to devalue or discount communication and depend on clear power structures. They are seen as less cohesive and adaptable (Alexander & Lupfer, 1987) than are healthy families.

Roles in the family may well be one of the most significant factors contributing to sexual abuse, probably more significant than specific sexual arousal or satisfaction issues. In healthy families, we see a boundary between adults and children. This boundary may be explicit (parents draw the rules and that's that) or more implicit (family meetings and logical consequences). The boundary is clear regardless of an authoritarian or permissive or democratic style.

In dysfunctional families, one of the symptoms that we see is a lack, or distortion of, a boundary. Specifically, abusive families show three patterns of boundary breakdown.

1. *Dictatorial/possessive father*. In this pattern, the father figure is in a position of ultimate control. This is more than an authoritarian style; it is one in which the spouse and children are seen equally as possessions or objects. Once the spouse is pushed over the boundary into equal status with the children, the possibility is set up for the father to sexually abuse any (or all) of the children. He clearly sees this as his right and will frequently find it difficult to see any harm in the situation. The secrecy factor is strong in the family, and sexual contact between father and children may be of long duration. This pattern is illustrated in Case Study A in chapter 5 of this book.

2. *Immature/irresponsible father*. In this pattern, the father figure is typically a dependent personality who has shown some difficulty with responsible adult behavior. There may be a pattern of work instability, substance abuse/dependence, relationship difficulties, and general lack of appropriate control over his life. The spouse may either be a strong woman who has shown independent survival patterns or she may match the dependent patterns of her spouse. Passive-aggressive patterns are typical in either partner. Here, the father crosses the boundary as he becomes like one of the children in his irresponsibility. Again, a false equality is set up and the father sees a "permission" to have sexual contact with a child, most frequently the oldest daughter. This pattern is rein-

forced in a blended family where the supposed "incest taboo" is weaker. The first sexual contact may precipitate other symptoms such as increased substance abuse or significant depression in the father and withdrawal or runaway behavior in the child. It is this symptomatology that, fortunately, increases the possibility of a report. (See Case Study B.)

3. *Pseudoadult child.* This pattern may well exist in combination with the above, but is unique in that it is the child who crosses the boundary with pseudoadult behavior. Beyond typical "oldest child" patterns, the child (again generally the oldest daughter) goes past the role of "assistant mother" to become substitute mother/spouse. In some of the literature, this child is described as "parentified." This role may be enhanced by an actual or presumed disability on the mother's part such as illness or absence. The child takes on the family chores (cooking, cleaning, laundry, child care of siblings) and, implicitly, the role of pleasing the father. This may initially include cooking his favorite meal (at least as well as Mom) and progress to neck massage, leg or back massage, and "accidental" genital contact. Because this is a powerful role, the child frequently experiences strong emotional conflict and guilt around the report of the abuse. The report may well happen when this maternal child sees actual or potential sexual contact between the father and a sibling. The child in this role may almost completely lose the opportunity to go through the developmental stages of childhood. (See Case Study C.)

Each of these patterns sets up a false equality and sets the stage for abusive behavior. Because the whole family has been involved in setting up these patterns, the question of family, rather than offender, responsibility is sometimes raised. Statements like "Mom pushed him to do it with her nagging," "Susie liked the attention and encouraged it," or "Everybody knew about it and nobody did anything about it," frequently are used as rationalizations or minimizations by the offender and the whole family. So, who's the real bad guy?

It may be helpful to look at two different kinds of responsibility. This concept is difficult for some counselors to understand unless they have strong family systems training. First and foremost, the offender assumes 100% of the responsibility for the sexual contact. As the adult, he is the one that crosses the line, regardless of the reaction of the child. This is important to emphasize—*one hundred percent!*

There is a separate responsibility that the entire family has in establishing the patterns and atmosphere that existed at the time of abuse. They are responsible for those patterns, whether or not abuse actually occurs. The parents bear responsibility for their marital relationship and their parenting behaviors. Each bears responsibility for his or her share of the family financial and household management. The children, to an appropriately lesser degree, have their own responsibility for their share of family functioning. Accepting this notion of family (corporate) responsibility allows the counselor to enlist the whole family in mutual empowerment and responsibility for changing the maladaptive patterns. This responsibility is, in fact, a major positive force rather than an issue of fault or blame, and allows for significant systemic change.

Individual Dynamics

The one area that consistently begs for more research is the understanding of individual dynamics of the offender. The need for this information in treatment is even overshadowed by the need for objective information that would be useful in investigations, prosecution, sentencing and, generally, risk management. Prosecutors and judges need clear, objective information that indicates that Offender A is a high-risk rapist who should go to prison for 40 years, but Offender B is a low-risk intrafamilial abuser who should be given probation with treatment.

Thus far, the criminal justice system has utilized evaluations performed by court personnel, independent contractors, or evaluator-consultants hired by one side or the other in an adversarial style. The typical expectations of these evaluations may be anything from evidentiary (does the accused fit a "profile" of offenders), to risk of recidivism to risk on probation to "benefit" from incarceration. Typical evaluations include a clinical evaluation, the Minnesota Multiphasic Personality Inventory (MMPI), personality questionnaire, sex history, psychophysiological measures, and other assorted psychodiagnostic tools.

One would think that by this time clinicians would have amassed a vast database to help us make some predictions. Yes and no! Although data are there, we are hampered by a lack of consistent taxonomy or even agreement on variables (Levin & Stava, 1987). Levin and Stava, in reviewing MMPI research, report that, "Given the amount of MMPI research performed, the yield regarding knowledge of the personality of the sex offender seems rather sparse. In general, negative or inconsistent findings outweigh those of a positive nature" (p. 68). They report that rapists and forceful pedophiles show similar profiles of social alienation, hostility, and peculiarities of thought, and that pedophilic tendencies may somehow be associated with a "strong and rather rigid superego." They also conclude from both MMPI and non-MMPI research that "rapists and pedophiles are guilt-ridden individuals who attempt to inhibit expressions of aggression." There were no conclusions clearly speaking to other pedosexual offenders.

Clinical experience with regressed offenders shows little consistency regarding DSM-IIIR Axis I diagnoses except for depressive symptoms that may be reactive to the report and the legal process. Axis II disorders seem to focus on dependent and passive-aggressive personalities with immaturity and, to a lesser extent, antisocial tendencies. Borderline personality disorders also may be seen. Occupationally, these offenders range from clergy to cowboy, from truckers to police, from military to mechanics, from teachers to (yes) counselors.

Clearly, given current limitations, professionals must accept pedosexual offenders as a heterogeneous group with few similarities. We cannot at this time defend a single "profile." We are forced to put this part of the jigsaw puzzle together uniquely each time.

Legal Issues and the Criminal Justice System

Like everything else in the pedosexual arena, the legal system is usually seen as a complex obstacle for the counselor. Most counselors' thoughts about becoming a part of the legal labyrinth range from cautious curiosity to paranoia. Counselors trained in conflict resolution, mediation, and a "win-win," "I'm OK, you're OK" philosophy have a significant problem dealing with the adversarial judicial system.

Counselors who are confronted with sexual abuse will, however, have to deal with at least some elements of the system. It is helpful, and in some cases essential, to have a general understanding of the roles the counselor may play in a given setting and what a typical chronology might look like. This information should be general enough to be accurate regardless of jurisdiction, but procedures and statutes do vary, and the reader is certainly encouraged to obtain legal consultation. The reader is also referred to other resource books regarding strategies for testimony, record keeping, and so forth.

Roles

When working with sexual abuse, the counselor may play one or more roles. The most frequent task is to provide information, either formally or informally. There are two occasions for formal information: the report process (more about that later) and serving as a witness. Essentially, in these two formal areas, the counselor is like any other citizen and may be called upon to report what he or she has directly observed or heard from a student or client. Privileged communication or confidentiality may not be applicable. Information may be presented in a taped interview, written report, deposition, or court testimony.

Informal information sharing may include cooperating with an investigation or providing ongoing progress reports on victims or offenders in treatment to various agencies (child protective services, probation, juvenile court, etc.). The client should be informed as to what information will be shared, and with whom. Whenever possible, a release form should be signed.

Another role that counselors, particularly child counselors, must assume is that of advocate. Some jurisdictions may even court-appoint individuals or panels as advocates. Beyond being a witness, this person ensures that the client's interests are addressed appropriately in both the legal and treatment systems, including foster care. This appointed advocate may be (should request to be) invited to attend staffings, hearings, trials, and the like. In addition, courts may appoint a legal advocate (attorney) for the child(ren).

The counselor may also be called to testify as an expert witness. The expert witness may have different rules regarding testimony. For example, the expert witness is generally the only one who is permitted to express an opinion and can report hearsay evidence. The expert will have to be stipulated as such by the court (with possible challenge by one of the "sides"). The expert witness may either be seen as "independent" (all sides agreeing to accept the information) or as a consultant to one or more parties (in which the information probably will be viewed as helpful to the side that hires the consultant). In the latter situation, the counselor/consultant is compelled to the highest standards of ethical conduct regarding objectivity and concern about the current and potential victims. The expert may testify regarding an evaluation, treatment, or more general information, sometimes even without having seen the party involved. In some circumstances, the expert may be asked to provide a written report in lieu of, or in addition to, testimony.

Settings

There are generally four different settings or forums in which the counselor may appear: criminal, juvenile, family, or civil court. If the offender is being prosecuted for a criminal offense, the case will be heard in criminal (or superior) court. The counselor could be asked for information during investigation, preliminary hearing (or grand jury), trial, or sentencing mitigation hearing. The victim may also have to testify at any or all of those, although the courts have been moving toward keeping such appearances to a minimum.

Juvenile court may be involved in several ways. If the offender is a juvenile, the case may be prosecuted and go to trial in the offender's jurisdiction. Juvenile court may have different rules of evidence and, generally, more latitude may be given to the counselor who is testifying, particularly in the area of recommendations. The counselor may report on evaluations or the progress of treatment of either the child or the parents. A typical case for juvenile court originates through a dependency petition where the state, working through child protective services, may ask for custody of a victim and, possibly, siblings. This custody may be physical (the state removes the child from the home and places him or her into a shelter or foster care) or nonphysical (the child remains at home but the state can mandate treatment, control visits, etc.). Rules will be specified for judicial review, for example, at 30- or 90-day intervals. Families will be advised of their rights and have the right to be legally represented, as does the child. In some cases, juvenile court may be asked to rule on severance, the relinquishment or termination of parental rights that gives the state permanent custody and enables an adoption process.

More and more sexual abuse cases are being heard in family, conciliation, or divorce court. The phenomenon of allegations of abuse during custody fights is relatively new. Even though criminal charges may not be filed, custody and visitation decisions may be based on allegations made by the children. This arena is often the most difficult for the counselor because it produces the largest number of false allegations (Spiegel, 1988). Children may be coached or coerced into making or recanting stories or taking events out of context (MacFarlane, 1986). One parent also may attempt to alienate the children from the other parent (Gardner, 1987).

The least likely setting for the disposition of sexual abuse cases is civil court. Based on the increasing amount of litigation being heard, however, there could well be an increase in this arena. It could certainly become more common for a person who is not charged criminally for one reason or another to be sued for damages. In a recent case in which I consulted, the parents of a victim sued the parents of a juvenile offender for damages. There will, undoubtedly, be more of these cases.

The Process

It may be helpful to put this information into a chronology of a typical case to clarify the critical points for intervention or advocacy.

1. *The initial report.* All states have mandatory reporting laws regarding child abuse, particularly for school and health-related personnel. There is, typically, a release from liability for those who make a report in good faith, and increasingly severe penalties for failure to report even suspected abuse. Mandatory reporting transcends any client/patient confidentiality. (For a discussion of therapeutic issues regarding the report, see the chapter on victim intervention.) If the counselor works for a system or agency that has specific procedures for reporting abuse to others in the system, like a supervisor or principal, it still remains the ethical and probably the legal duty of the counselor to *ensure* that the report is made. The report may either be made to a child protective agency or to law enforcement. In many jurisdictions, the report will be automatically shared between those two agencies.

2. *The investigation.* Child protective services or the appropriate law enforcement agency will investigate the report. Frequently cases are handled on a priority basis. Sexual abuse cases are lower on the priority list than cases where there is an immediate risk of death or injury, but usually they are relatively high on the list. Some states have mandated timeframes in which a report must be investigated. Investigators will, of course, want any information about the abuse, but also may ask questions about general adjustment regarding the child or family. *Let the investigators investigate!* That is *not* the counselor's job.

3A. *Prosecution.* The prosecutor (county or district or state attorney) will decide whether to formally charge an alleged offender. There also may be a discussion of a plea bargain at this point. The plea bargain is an agreement where the offender pleads guilty or no contest to one or more charges in return for dismissal of other charges, expecting a reduced sentence.

3B. *CPS.* At the same time the prosecution decision is being made, CPS, with court approval, decides whether or not to remove a child. In many cases, it will encourage the offender to leave the home (it may or may not be able to *order* that) in order to leave the child there. CPS is frequently forced to make critical decisions based on protection of the child in a short period of time.

4. *Pretrial.* If there is a decision to prosecute, the offender will be arraigned. He will plead innocent, and a decision will be made whether to release him, and whether he will be released with or without bond. An attorney will be appointed if necessary. There will then be either a preliminary hearing or grand jury to decide if there is enough evidence to proceed to trial, and an indictment, or formal charges, will be filed.

5. *Trial.* If there is no plea bargain, the case will proceed to trial. Unfortunately, this is often a lengthy process. It may well be to everyone's benefit to plea bargain to avoid trial. Physical evidence may be sparse, and conviction for sexual abuse, particularly with young children, may be difficult.

6. *Sentencing.* Whether sentencing results from conviction by trial or plea bargaining, it is usually another critical point for the counselor. Typically a presentencing investigation is held to determine appropriateness of probation versus incarceration. The victim may well be asked for input at this time. In some states, with mandatory sentencing laws, the judge may have limited latitude. Jurisdictions vary in their sentencing from straight probation (usually with mandatory treatment) to probation and jail (maybe in a work release program) to prison incarceration with or without chance of parole.

7. *Probation.* Offenders, either adult or juvenile, may be placed on probation. Generally, probation is an alternative to prison, whereas parole is a monitoring process after release from prison. Probation requirements may vary considerably regarding frequency of reports, treatment mandates, restrictions on visitation or contact with minors, alcohol consumption, and other issues. The counselor, whether in a primary or supportive role, will need to coordinate closely with the probation officer (P.O.) regarding mutual expectations and roles. The counselor will also have to communicate clearly those expectations and roles to the client. There should be a written agreement indicating the limits of confidentiality. The counselor will probably need to report attendance, general progress, risk assessment, family progress, fee payment, and violations of probation conditions. The probation officer will probably be on the treatment team and attend staffings (meetings of the treatment team). Additionally, he or she may require periodic written or verbal reports for significant decisions like visitation, termination

of treatment, or family reunification. The P.O. usually also wants to maintain contact with the victim and the victim's counselor/ therapist even though he or she may not be legally mandated to do that.

The legal process and criminal justice system present a real challenge for many counselors. The counselor's knowledge of the system is beneficial to the client, who will be looking for support and answers to the understandable feelings of confusion. This knowledge also is important so that appropriate therapeutic interventions can be made, the subject of chapters 2–4.

CHAPTER 2

INTERVENTION STRATEGIES—VICTIM

Diagnosis and treatment planning generally seems to be a fairly straightforward process—gather symptoms, check out hypotheses, make a diagnosis, plan treatment to deal with symptoms or underlying problem, and reevaluate. Counselors who work with children know how tricky the process can be when dealing with short attention spans, limited verbal ability, and idiopathic perceptions of the world. Complicate that picture with sexual abuse and the counselor faces a real challenge.

Rather than use symptomatology in its usual way, this section will focus on "the picture" of the sexually abused child at three age periods—the young child (younger than 7 years old), the middle child (7 to puberty), and the adolescent—and will present intervention strategies appropriate to each of those periods. Unless noted, the pictures and strategies will apply to either sex. In the first two age periods, we will assume that the intervention is taking place within 1 year of the last abusive incident. In the adolescent period, we will discuss delayed intervention as well.

The counselor working with the child may be either in a primary or supportive role. The interventions discussed can be used in both situations, but the supportive counselor also has the responsibility for coordinating with the primary counselor/therapist.

The Young Child

Perhaps the most important perspective in dealing with young children is a developmental one. It is essential for counselors to have a good understanding of normal psychosexual development as well as cognitive and social development. This is particularly essential with young children because of their verbal limitations.

Young children are eager to please and will answer "yes" to many questions inappropriately. Answers may not be organized and may seem tangential or, in fact, may be lies, especially to avoid punishment. Children also are egocentric and may well have difficulty dealing with strangers (Waterman, 1986).

For an in-depth treatment of early childhood psychosexual development, the reader is referred to Yates (1978). Children are curious about male-female differences, physically and in regard to sex roles. Masturbation is typical and may be more overt in girls at this age. Although "humping" behavior is not unusual, the exact nature of coitus (penile-vaginal penetration) is only rarely known. In fact, if there is any notion of penetration, anal intercourse seems much more logical to the young child.

With this brief summary of development, we are a bit better prepared to look at the picture of the sexually abused young child. Two general characteristics are important in that picture: fear and adult-type sexual knowledge.

Fear may be shown directly in terms of withdrawal or indirectly in the form of nightmares and night terrors. Withdrawal may be expressed against people in general, strangers, or men. The trauma may come from a wide variety of sources and, at this age, some sexual abuse actually may not be very traumatic. Because young children do not, almost by definition, know that sexual behavior is "bad," the physical sensations may feel good, particularly in a nurturing situation like bathing or play. It may well be that physical pain or discomfort may be more traumatic, whether or not it is associated with sexual contact.

The issue of a child's fear of, or withdrawal from, strangers may be difficult for the counselor, and establishing trust is critical in evaluation or treatment. The counselor must provide a sense of warmth, caring, and respect for the child while still maintaining a clearly adult role. Fortunately, most counselors dealing with this age group are experienced with these issues and need only give extra attention to trust if there is an indication of abuse.

The presence of atypical knowledge of sex is another less-than-perfect indicator of abuse. It can be helpful to the counselor, however, if he or she is really able to see the knowledge or behavior as *adult*-type behavior. Let's look at examples of child, marginal (child/adult), and adult behavior.

Typical child behaviors include giggling about toileting, anatomical curiosity (playing doctor), touching of others' genitals, and masturbation. Language is simple and, perhaps, repetitive (ca-ca, pee-pee, weenie, poo-poo, gina, boobies, tinkle, poop).

These behaviors become marginal when adult activity, motivation, or language is indicated—digital penetration, extended stroking of genitals, coercion/persuasion, or genital kissing. As mentioned, perhaps through exposure to such sources as cable TV, children do engage in "humping" either with or without clothes, but no awareness of the penetration involved is usually present. Marginal language includes "fuck (as a descriptive rather than expletive term), lay, cock, pussy, suck, bang." Any of these types of behavior or language would certainly warrant added attention and concern.

Adult behavior should really raise some "red flags." Included in this category would be oral-genital contact, penile penetration (or clear attempt at penetration), oral-breast contact, and open-mouth kissing. Language includes "screw, butt-fuck, rimming, fisting, eat out, blow-job." Chances are that these behaviors were learned by either close observations of adults, extended exposure to sexually explicit media, or sexual abuse.

The Report

Dealing with children younger than 7 years old poses some unique problems regarding the report to authorities and the legal process in general. The basic premise, of course, is that a report is necessary for the protection of the child. Because a report is usually mandated for suspicion of abuse as well as clear evidence, the counselor may be obligated to report with only a minimal level of certainty regarding actual abuse.

The temptation is perhaps strongest with this age range to continue to push for more information either before or after the report—in other words, to become part of the investigation. This temptation generally should be resisted for two reasons: it can easily create confusion for the child and seriously jeopardize/sabotage the prosecutor's case. The latter occurs if there is any hint of leading questions, evaluator bias, or, even, encouragement for the child to talk about abuse. If the counselor needs to pursue an assessment/ evaluation (perhaps if asked to do so by the investigation team), extra preparation is necessary through reading, workshops, or video training. The reader is specifically referred to MacFarlane and Waterman (1986).

Certainly a sense of frustration pervades the investigation phase. Even if the child gives some clear signals during an assessment, prosecutors may be reluctant to go to trial without physical evidence (there typically isn't any), relying solely on the testimony of this young a child. Some new legal developments, including the increased acceptance of videotaped evidence, may be highly significant (MacFarlane & Waterman, 1986).

Early Treatment Phase

In older children within the younger-than-7 age group, the early treatment phase would be focused on crisis intervention. With this age group, however, the primary concern is trust and rapport-building.

Whenever possible, the counselor should use the child's mother as a bridge in helping to build trust. This may be a slight deviation from the way the counselor would treat a nonabused child. Clearly, the counselor would not be able to utilize the mother in cases where she is suspected of involvement in the abuse. Caution also should be taken in a case where the mother is still in a stage of denial regarding the veracity of the report or is blaming the child. The mother can help by the following steps.

1. *Preparing the child.* The child can be told that she or he is going to a nice, pleasant place to meet a new grown-up who talks and plays with kids. The mother has, ideally, had a chance previously to meet the counselor so she can describe this new grown-up with one or two specifics (this grown-up has a nice smile, or talks softly, or has a soft rug). This can be done in a rather factual way (not overly trying to convince the child). If the child asks why they are visiting, the mother may simply say that they're going to talk about how things are going in the family. If asked directly, the mother should not lie about the abuse concerns.

2. *Accompanying the child.* The mother can encourage the child to bring a favorite toy or object (teddy bear, doll). Mother can stay with the child through the first session and as many of the subsequent sessions as the counselor deems helpful.

3. *Supporting the child.* It seems almost silly to think that a mother would not support her child. It would not be unusual, however, for a highly stressed mother in the beginning stages of

the abuse crisis unintentionally to meet her own needs first. One way this is manifested is for the mother to get into the role of investigator (asking the famous "why" questions) or feeling caught in the trap between spouse and children, a highly energy-consuming position. As a result, the child may get some protection, but also perceives the chaos in the family, and may feel a lot of the mother's ambivalence or rage toward the father. The essence of support for the child is to give permission to feel—that it is, in fact, OK for the child to act like a child and to be frightened, confused, and unpredictable. The mother will also want to resist the temptation to act as therapist; that is, to get involved in the details of the abuse and to draw conclusions from play activities or verbal cues. As mentioned, of course, the mother may be in denial, which makes the support more difficult but, perhaps, even more important.

4. *Being there.* During a crisis like abuse, probably the child's biggest fear is abandonment. The message the child perceives is that because there is so much chaos, either or both parents might just leave to escape the problems. This fear is obviously aggravated if there has been, or may be, a divorce, if father has moved out, or if there have been loud or violent arguments.

5. *Therapy.* Mother might also help the child, and herself, by agreeing to individual therapy if indicated. Frequently, she will have many issues and feelings that would be more appropriately addressed outside her child's counseling sessions.

The Therapeutic Atmosphere

In both the early and ongoing phases of treatment with the young child, the counselor's most important task may be in creating an atmosphere for trust building. This atmosphere includes the physical environment as well as the counselor's behavior.

The physical environment should be simple but clearly focused on the young child. It could be an office or playroom as long as it provides warmth and comfort for the child including child-sized furniture, pillows, or a clean, comfortable carpet (as long as the counselor feels comfortable there). There should be a *small* selection of simple toys available—blocks, puppets, soft dolls (anatomically correct are preferred), doll house (or other ways to portray a family), paper of various sizes with large crayons or markers, and clay/playdough. A sand tray/box is beneficial if the room allows. A larger selection than this will shorten the attention span, diffuse the play, and reduce contact with the counselor. If there is a large space, the "kid's special part" should be clearly defined.

The counselor's behavior is more critical than the physical environment. The young child should be approached with gentleness but without condescending baby talk. Several minutes should be spent with the mother and child together in the waiting area. The counselor can bring an object (stuffed animal, puppet) to meet the child or can acknowledge a like object if the child has brought one. Initial focus should be on anything "special" about the child— the toy, colorful clothing, big smile, and so forth. This allows the child's egocentricity to be experienced as OK. The child should be approached from a basically equal height—sitting next to the child, and squatting or sitting while the child stands—in order to avoid the rather threatening sense of an adult looming over the child. Above all, the child can relate to a *gentle* humor focusing on the "child" part of the counselor ("sometimes adults like to do things like play with blocks or sit on the floor," "that's a silly looking horse I drew, it looks like a hippopotamus") and, *at the same time*, acknowledgment of the child's achievements ("that's a great block tower," "what neat colors"). Both approaches emphasize the equality (basic OK-ness) of both the child and adult without a false front.

Ongoing Treatment

Duration of treatment for young children may vary from short-term (less than 6 months) to longer term (over a year) depending on the level of trust achieved and the overall stability in the child's life (foster placement, stability of parents, etc.) (Long, 1986).

Long (1986) has done a good job of adapting Sgroi's (Porter, Blick, & Sgroi, 1982) treatment issues for victims of sexual abuse to the younger population. These are summarized in the following list.

1. *"Damaged goods" syndrome.* This refers to self-, familial, and societal perception of the child as different, used, pitiful, vulnerable and maybe, as we discussed earlier, partly to blame. Young children see the sexual contact as so dissonant or incongruous that they ask even more than the usual number of unproductive "why" questions.
2. *Guilt.* Although the young child does not feel the same guilt or shame as an older child would, egocentricity leads to the conclusion that she or he is the cause of all the chaos and confusion in the home, absence of father, and "strange" reactions of mother.

3. *Fear.* As mentioned, fear of abandonment is the primary fear for this age group.
4. *Depression.* Although withdrawal is usually related to anxiety, it can also be an indication of depression, as can somatic complaints (particularly stomach pain), listlessness, and "spacey" behavior.
5. *Low self-esteem and poor social skills.* I would modify this slightly to focus more on perceived powerlessness and helplessness. The child can either go into withdrawal behavior or become an extremely powerful child in the sense of bossiness or highly controlling behavior in dealing with either peers or adults.
6. *Repressed anger and hostility.* Although some young children do not experience anger because of the context of the abuse, some do experience and repress anger. Anger may be directed at mother as well as the offender.
7. *Inability to trust.* This may well be the most important issue, particularly in intrafamilial abuse. It may be aggravated by the duration of the contact and the amount of physical pain or discomfort experienced.
8. *Blurred role boundaries and role confusion.* As mentioned in the previous discussion of family dynamics, the child can perceive significant problems as to who is in charge of the family and who is responsible for protection. This also reemphasizes the importance of the mother in the recovery process as a strong, protective person.
9. *Pseudomaturity and failure to complete developmental tasks.* This is related to the power issues noted previously. The child is put into an inappropriately powerful role and does not move through developmental stages in sequence. This includes issues of sexualization, but also affects physical, cognitive, and affective development.
10. *Self-mastery and control.* The child feels no sense of control or options. Regaining these options will be an important goal of treatment.

In addition to these 10 areas, Long (1986) identified 5 more issues specific to treating the young child: importance of teaming with the child's mother, inappropriate attachment behavior, infantile regressive behavior, need for body contact and body awareness, and need for education about feelings. We already have discussed the issue of teaming with the mother.

The issue of inappropriate attachment is particularly important in this stage of ongoing treatment. Once the issues of trust in the early stage of treatment are successfully handled, it is easy for the child to become extremely attached to the counselor. The counselor may be one of the few people who has really listened to and respected the child and his or her feelings. Even when the child expresses considerable anger, fear, or sadness in a session, the child really comes to value the time with the counselor and sees the counselor as nurturing. This overlaps into the issue regarding body contact and awareness because the counselor can become an important model for appropriate, nonexploitive, and fully consensual touching. Pats on the shoulder and back and hugs of greeting and leaving are positive. The child may well push this limit, however, and want to sit on the counselor's lap or want to maintain constant physical contact during conversation or play. Counselors should be aware of this and establish a comfortable limit; for example, lap-sitting only briefly, if at all, and encouragement to play independently and creatively with more verbal interactions from the counselor. The counselor also should be aware of the child's natural tendency to test limits and to move rather quickly from "affectionate" attachment to powerful testing behaviors such as hitting, drawing on the wall instead of the paper, or wanting to use "adult toys" such as the telephone or an answering machine.

The tendency toward infantile regression is important to observe. Young children will frequently regress, not only in response to a fearful situation but, more indirectly, to express their need for nurturance, comfort, and security. The counselor's office or playroom may be a safe place to be able to "act like a baby" and cuddle up for hugs and protection, perhaps with some thumb-sucking. The child can be permitted to engage in this behavior and also be encouraged to move on to more developmentally appropriate interaction.

Affective awareness is a major issue at any age within this age group. At this age, the child should be aware of basic feelings and be able to label them. There are many techniques for teaching this, with children reacting quite well to simple happy face drawings or to illustrations of children and adults in child-oriented books.

It may seem that this stage of treatment deals only indirectly with the abuse issues. Remember that one of our philosophical assumptions was that "treatment is prevention." That is particularly true at this age. Overemphasis on details of the abuse may be counterproductive because it may focus on the child's vulnerability and weakness rather than on an appropriate sense of power and control. It may also seem illogical to the young child who has repressed the abuse in order to move on developmentally to several new tasks and concerns.

Group work, specifically a young child's play group, may be a helpful adjunct to treatment. Children develop trust with other children and find out that they aren't different. Obviously, this option may not even be available to some counselors, depending on the number and age of their clients.

Play groups can be positive in terms of appropriate social skill development, particularly if sexualization has resulted in significant sexual acting out. They can also resolve the typical problem of isolation in sexual abuse victims. Power issues also can be addressed. Play groups may even become the primary treatment modality in a longer range plan. When play groups are used, care should be given to creating a small group of a homogeneous age. At this age, mixed groups of boys and girls are appropriate. Placement should be continually reevaluated.

The participation of parents, particularly mother, in the play group process is crucial. Some models include the mother directly in the group itself on a continuing basis, and others use an alternate group format (children seen for 2 or 3 weeks, then mothers seen in a group). Damon and Waterman (1986) presented a parallel play group model, in which children and mothers meet in separate groups at the same time, each dealing with a predetermined, structured task (saying "no," body awareness, etc.). These approaches strongly emphasize the mother-child bonding process.

Empowerment and Termination

Although empowerment was mentioned in the list of treatment issues during the ongoing phase, it should be clearly reemphasized during the last stage of treatment. Even when the child has successfully resolved the major issues of treatment, whether they be fear, withdrawal, anger, or sexualization, he or she remains more vulnerable to further abuse or exploitation than the "average" child. Before termination is complete, an educational/therapeutic approach can be used to improve the child's appropriate sense of power and, therefore, self-defense. The following behaviors are an indication of empowerment.

1. *The ability to seek help.* This includes asking mother, teachers, siblings, or adult relatives for help in any situation where the child feels helpless. It also includes asking for help from the counselor and, as part of the termination process, a strong agreement to return for more sessions when necessary. The child can be given a business card to put in a special place and encouraged to call the counselor in the future, "just to say hi." It is amazing how often children respond to this suggestion.

2. *The ability to say "no."* Even the most well-intentioned parent cringes when facing the possibility of his or her 4-year-old actually being more negative than the child is already. Of course, the ability to say "no" to inappropriate touch is specific and does not usually result in the child becoming more generally negative. In fact, the child with strong self-esteem is less likely to engage in limit-testing and more likely to sense the power in accepting responsibility. Protection should be taught regarding people within the family as well as "stranger danger."

3. *The ability to express feelings.* The child should be able to identify feelings more clearly and have a sense of permission that expressing feelings will be accepted by the adults the child knows.

The presence of these behaviors in the child will certainly help the counselor to feel more comfortable about the termination process, but it still may be a difficult time *for the counselor.* Counselors, particularly those who are relatively inexperienced, may well have the more difficult time in letting go. Having seen themselves as the rescuers and protectors of the child, they run the risk of wondering if the child is going to be vulnerable in their absence. Because children form strong attachments, the counselors also feel significant and understandable loss.

The goodbye process should focus on reassurances that the counselor will "be there." Other counselors or staff who have related with the child should also reassure the child that they will be there as well (or in case the primary counselor is unavailable). An exchange of small gifts or tokens (a drawing or card) is helpful in the reassurance process.

The Young Male Victim

As noted earlier, the observations and strategies for the young child are appropriate for both male and female victims. A few additional comments on the young male victim may be helpful.

More than any other age group, the young boy is seen as similar to the girl. Offenders report seeing the young child as attractive because there is a nonspecific sexuality; that is, both sexes look very much the same. There is also less fear of homosexuality for the offender because he can rationalize that the young boy doesn't look at all like a male adult.

The boy victim presents himself for therapy much like the girl. There may be a somewhat greater tendency for acting-out, limit-testing, or overactive behavior. There also may be more extreme swings or exaggerations during treatment—more overt affection as well as more rebellion.

At this age, there is frequently a question of preference for the sex of the counselor. Although a male counselor may well be effective as a role model to show that men can be sensitive and nonabusive, the boy may still feel more comfortable with a female counselor, particularly in the early stages of treatment. If at all possible, the child should have contact with at least one male counselor who is on the treatment team. This may be the parents' counselor or a colleague of the primary counselor. The play group is an especially valuable opportunity for appropriate male models.

In general, the young victim clearly influences counselors' emotions and motivation as healers. Counselors want to make all victims better and do it quickly. They have to recognize that children do not, however, work on their timetable. Fortunately, there is a good chance for a significant positive interaction at this young age. Because the treatment of sexual abuse is such a new phenomenon in many ways, it may take some time for counselors to see the role that they have played in preventing further abuse.

The Middle Child

In terms of numbers, counselors will most likely be dealing with this population group of age 7 to puberty. As their efforts at prevention and education improve, they hope to shorten the time between incident and report. Because they know that the largest number of cases are initiated in this prepubertal age group, there should even be a significant increase in the number of children counselors will be seeing.

Why is this age group so "popular" among offenders? Why don't offenders prefer the adolescent "nubile" bodies that are so strongly associated with arousal in movies and TV? Why aren't they more turned on by adult development and turned off by the lack of it? I caught you asking "why" questions again.

The questions are, of course, puzzling, especially if we are thinking logically about arousal issues. We will explore these issues in more depth in our discussion of the offender. Suffice it to say at this point that issues of power and control may be much stronger issues than sexual arousal. The "attractiveness" of the 7-to-puberty age group may be a combination of enough maturity to interact verbally and, therefore, present a false image of consensuality, and, yet, very little real power in relationship to adults, particularly within the family. The child will usually assume that the parent is "right" and, at least initially, accept the abuse, despite pain, discomfort, or a clear sense that it is "wrong." Some of the best examples of this are shown in how many children react to the first attempt at inappropriate touching: silence, feigning sleep, or denial that the touch happened.

Again, as for the young child, it is helpful for us to keep developmental issues in mind in working with the middle child. How is this age group different from the younger group we have just discussed?

Perhaps the most identifiable difference for the counselor is the dramatically improved verbal communication. The older child is more fluent and understandable, able to order syntax and, generally, correctly order events and objects in time and space. There is also an improved ability to articulate affect, although this may be an area of concern for the abused child.

The middle child is more in touch with the self in relationship to others and has lost some, but not all, of the earlier egocentricity. The sense of security has broadened to accommodate increased independence. There is a better sense of family beyond the mother-child bond, and a better sense of bonding with the father or father-figure. There is also a sense of loyalty and, critical to the problem of sexual abuse, the ability to keep a secret.

The Report

By this time, we've all learned what signs and symptoms of sexual abuse to look for in the age group of the middle child. The clearest signs are ones we don't usually see, the physical signs: genital irritation, bruising, or swelling; urinary burning; recurrent or sudden-onset encopresis or enuresis; and vaginal or rectal bleeding or discharge. Most abuse, of course, causes little visible harm. As prosecutors will tell you, there is typically little physical evidence.

We've also seen the list of psychological/behavioral signs and symptoms: behavioral acting out, poor academics, withdrawal, running away, substance use/abuse, peer problems, difficulty relating to men, wanting to stay away from home, and so forth. Unfortunately, this is pretty close to the same list we've seen for learning disabilities, depression, substance abuse, and a host of other difficulties. What are some unique behaviors that show up for the abused child? Two particular areas stand out: the pressure to keep the secret, and sexual or sexually related behavior. These two frequently provide "the picture."

If you ask most children what their parents do for a living, how many are in their family, or how many rooms there are in their home, you'll probably get a quick, if sometimes inaccurate, answer. The abused child (in this case, a victim of any form of abuse) will look at you with a slightly glazed look and either stammer out a response or ask you why you want to know. Although "the secret" is not always so obvious, we should not underestimate the amount of energy it takes to keep it. The child may well become more distractable, lose interest in school, and move away from peers who might have been considered friends. Peers, in fact, may be an important part of the picture because they will notice significant behavioral changes before adults do. As noted earlier, peers frequently become the source of a report because they will either detect a problem or elicit the truth from the victim and then report it either to their parents or to a teacher.

Sexual behavior remains a significant part of the picture, although we may be led astray by sexual language. Whereas language gives us some of our best clues in the case of the younger child, the middle child is normally likely to use rather explicit language, both as expletive and in reference to sexual relationships. Behavior, however, may still remain as good a clue as in the case of the younger child. Although exploratory behavior is still common, this age group is more likely to look for information from peers or from sexually explicit media rather than from physical contact. When physical contact does happen, it is again most likely to be touching, with little likelihood of either oral or vaginal penetration. If we see behavior more clearly sexual than this, it is a strong indicator of sexualization. Again, it is possible for sexualization to occur in the absence of abuse, if, for example, there has been extended exposure to sexually explicit media.

In female victims, one of the major indicators of sexual abuse is a sudden interest in boyfriends, and, particularly, boys who are 4–5 years older. Behavior in these pairs is remarkably inappropriate, with kissing and hand-holding at the younger end of this group, and extended kissing, genital stroking, and oral-genital contact at the older end of the spectrum.

Whether the counselor is the first to notice these signs or whether the report is received unexpectedly, the counselor may be one of the first adults to hear a report of sexual abuse. The counselor's tasks are basic: report the abuse and support the victim. Some counselors have expressed concern that the two tasks are antithetical, that the report to authorities destroys any counseling relationship. The report is necessary because:

1. It is the law. As mentioned previously, even if counselors are obliged to report to another person in a school or agency, they are still responsible for ensuring that the report is made. The child must see that the adults around him or her will follow the law.
2. The child can seek out other support but needs the protection of Child Protective Services or law enforcement first. Some counselors unintentionally develop a rather egocentric position that only they can help, understand, or communicate with a particular child.
3. With honesty and the focus on feelings, the counseling relationship can survive and prosper.

During the session in which the child divulges the abuse, support takes precedence over interrogation. There is a tendency to press for details, but they may neither be necessary nor helpful. The most essential details are the identity of the offender and clear time/date and behavior involved in one incident. Further interrogation may simply be confusing and put the child on the defensive. Again, let the investigators investigate! It is far more important to reassure the child of having done the right thing and accept the child's feelings of fear, anger, guilt, ambivalence, and confusion.

The child should be told that a report will be made. The younger child will easily understand this. The older child may well question confidentiality but usually understands the importance of the report; in fact, the report validates self-worth and the child's right to protection.

Protection is the primary focus of the time period around the report and it is not the counselor's role. It is the role of the child protective service or law enforcement. Regardless of the process used or the efficacy of "the system," it has the role and resources for protection.

How can the counselor assist "the system" in protecting the child? Primarily, the counselor's report should be an accurate description of the child's report. The counselor also may be present in a supportive role when the investigators question the child. The counselor also may provide helpful information regarding the child's behavior, peer relations, emotional adjustment, and family relationships. If the child remains in contact with the counselor after the report, the counselor then becomes a member of the treatment team and may even be identified as the primary therapist.

During the time of the report, there is a strong possibility that the counselor will be asked to deal with the veracity of the report. This will happen because the offender, at least initially, will almost certainly deny the allegation. Many adults will also choose to believe an adult over a child. The counselor may be one of the few adults that the child trusts, thus it is essential that the child be believed until there is a clear reason to the contrary. This is not to say that children never lie—that is clearly an oversimplification. It implies rather that the role of the counselor is to support the child, not investigate the allegations. Without denying the possible harm from false allegations, there is an even more pressing danger in allowing unreported abuse to continue. There is even reason to believe that the report alone may be one of the most important factors in the prevention of new abuse. Given that caveat, some guidelines relevant to veracity may be helpful.

1. Although children are not normally adept at describing sexual encounters that are fantasies, they can repeat things that they have been told in a very literal way. They do not, however, have the ability to describe behavior fully unless they have actually experienced it. Therefore, asking a child to describe a behavior in different words may be a helpful check against the possibility that the child may have read about or seen sexually explicit behavior. These media exposures may be superimposed on the actual abuse.

2. Children may lie if they fear punishment, especially if they feel, correctly or not, that they have done something wrong. They may, in fact, be more likely to deny an actual abuse than to create a fantasy abuse.

3. Because children have a strong need to please, it is essential for the counselor to avoid leading questions such as, "did Daddy touch you in your private parts?", for both reasons of accuracy and legal evidence.

4. Older children and adolescents may have power or revenge motivations for making a report, but these motivations are relatively rare and are usually dropped or changed dramatically once the consequences are clear. These are some of the most difficult cases to sort out.

Again, the role of the counselor during the report period is not to act as investigator or interrogator. In a sense, the child's counselor is in a unique position to be able to provide support regardless of the specific veracity or accuracy of the child's report. Whether the report is totally or partially true, an exaggeration, misunderstanding, or fantasy, the child will need support.

Crisis Intervention

Like in the entire treatment process, it is difficult to put a precise timeframe on the crisis intervention phase. In fact, crisis should be expected throughout the process.

It would not be a mistake to assume that every victim and every offender is a suicide risk. That risk should be the subject of one of the first evaluative judgments during the crisis stage. The difficulty of the report seems to be a major factor in evaluation. That is, the more emotional conflict involved, the higher the suicide risk. It is not unusual to see the child swing between report, recantation, and change because of this conflict, which leads to perceptions of rejection. With the child's typical egocentricity, the child perceives that the family's problems are caused by the report rather than the molestation, and thinks of suicide as a solution.

The suicide risk dramatically emphasizes the conflict the victim experiences, with alternating (and simultaneous) feelings of fear, guilt, and rage magnified by basic ambivalence. Rage is the easiest feeling for most adults to understand, but the most difficult for the child to express. We can empathize with the sense of violation, betrayal of trust, and secrecy. We expect and encourage the expression of rage to the point that we're surprised when it doesn't occur. For many children, of course, it is extremely difficult to reconcile their rage with the affection they may otherwise have felt, and with strong societal messages that children are supposed to do what parents say, even when they don't like it. The rage, in fact, may not truly surface for years.

The difficulty in reconciling rage overlaps with the guilt factor. The child initially is likely to feel that he or she is the one who did something "bad" or was a part of something bad. This is complicated in children who, at some level or at some occasions, enjoyed the attention, affection, or physical sensations of the sexual contact. The guilt may even intensify once the child experiences the upset subsequent to the report—his or her removal or father's removal, mother's frequent ambivalence, siblings' blame, and peers' questioning and curiosity. It may be easier for the child to express anger toward the mother than the offender.

Children may exhibit a range of fear behaviors. They may fear physical punishment from either parent, reinforced by direct or implied threat from the offender during the sexual contact. That threat also may induce fear of parental divorce ("If Mom finds out, she'll leave us") or maternal rejection ("Mom won't like you for doing this") and may be accompanied by the all-too-truthful statement that "Nobody will believe me anyway." This is compounded by the fear of the legal system (court appearance) and, later, fear of losing the father to prison. For the victim of extrafamilial contact, the fear of physical retribution may be more of an issue.

The key to dealing with the fear, guilt, and rage, particularly during the crisis stage, is to focus on "the child." These feelings are *all* "OK for kids" and *totally* acceptable. An *appropriate* sense of relative powerlessness helps to demonstrate their lack of blame, fault, and so forth while still leaving open the option that they can become more powerful *and* remain children developmentally. The theme of returning the victim to "normal" childhood will be repeated throughout the treatment process. At this point, the "permission" to feel is critical.

Ongoing Treatment

We will establish a framework for this longest phase of treatment by again looking at Sgroi's 10 "impact issues" (Porter, Blick, & Sgroi, 1982) as they apply to the age group of the middle child, and then proceed with some specific intervention strategies. We will focus particularly on the victims of intrafamilial abuse, and then will discuss separately any issues that apply specifically to other forms of pedosexual contact. The 10 impact and treatment issues are:

1. *"Damaged goods" syndrome.* This applies whether there has been any physical damage or not. It had been possible for us, in the past, to take some small comfort in the fact that most cases of sexual abuse did not result in major physical damage. Unfortunately, we may not be able to protect our children from the impact of AIDS. Although the percentage of AIDS cases attributable to abuse has been small so far, there is every reason to believe that the numbers, if not the percentage, will continue to increase. Regardless of physical injury, society and the child both label the sexualization experience as creating an oddity to be both pitied and feared. It is a typical crisis point, for example, when a victim/survivor reveals her experience to a serious boyfriend or girl friend or, later, a spouse.

2. *Guilt.* As mentioned, this is part of the great ambivalence most children feel. They feel responsible for the sexual behavior itself (especially if they enjoyed it and the offender reinforced that), responsible for the report (whether or not it came from them directly), and, certainly, responsible for the chaos in the family as a

result of the report. This is a recurring theme in treatment. We have seen it in the crisis intervention phase, and it continues to be a topic through individual and family work.

3. *Fear.* Like the young child, the middle child continues to feel a significant fear of abandonment, particularly if there has been a foster placement. The child fears, with some reality, that the mother may choose the father over her or him. The fear of punishment or retribution mentioned during the crisis intervention phase may continue for some time into treatment.

4. *Depression.* As noted, during the crisis intervention phase there is a suicide risk in many cases, and depression will continue, especially if there is a sense of rejection from either parent. The counselor needs to refocus continually on the child's feelings of need for self-affirmation and worth.

5. *Low self-esteem and poor social skills.* Again, I would prefer to focus on the child's feeling of powerlessness and lack of control. This feeling may be even more apparent in the middle child than it is in younger children. Verbal and physical limit-testing may be more severe and may include aggressive as well as sexual behavior. Although this behavior also may be linked to anger, there is a good chance it has more to do with compensating for a perceived lack of power and control. This type of behavior is frequently described as being unprovoked and may be directed at peers or siblings toward whom the child previously had related in a friendly manner.

6. *Repressed anger and hostility.* This is, obviously, the other side of the ambivalence issue. The anger tends to build up over a period of time, from possible initial acceptance to a sense of violated rage. This buildup may be one of the factors most closely related to the duration of the sexual contact. Much of this anger may be vented and handled more easily if there is an early report. On the other hand, if the report is never made, as in the case of an adult survivor to be discussed in detail later, the anger and rage issues may well be debilitating and highly resistant to treatment. It is also important to note that much, sometimes most, of the anger is directed at the mother for failing to protect the child or report the abuse. The child frequently assumes that the mother knew, or "must have known," about what was happening.

7. *Inability to trust.* This is more of an issue at this age because it may be harder for the middle child to regain the sense of trust. Again, there may be considerable lack of trust in the mother, and this relationship must be rebonded as soon as possible. There also may be greater difficulty with trust issues if the offender was the natural father or a stepfather of long duration. This lack of trust

frequently is generalized to all men and may continue on into adulthood, interfering with normal, positive relationships.

8. *Blurred role boundaries and role confusion.* This issue was described in the section on family dynamics and will receive additional attention as we look at the family treatment modality. If the child is not able to deal with this issue in the family context, the counselor will have to deal with it using role-play and other forms of substitutes.

9. *Pseudomaturity and failure to complete developmental tasks.* The abused child, particularly the oldest child, will easily assume a pseudoadult role in the family either because of the cause or the effect of the abuse. There may well be a parentification of one or more of the children. It would not be unusual for a 9-year-old to look behaviorally like age 15, 18, 25, or 30 at various times, and to be expected to move among those ages at the demand of the offender or the rest of the family. This is both a reflection of the sexualization (as it applies specifically to sexual roles and behavior) and the more general pseudomaturity.

A special note on sexualization issues is important here. As noted previously, sexualization is essentially a developmental issue. The extent of this developmental skip may be hard to predict. It is apparently not directly related to age, type of sexual behavior, or duration of the abuse. The only exception to this may be a relationship between the occurrence of penile-vaginal coitus and the extent of sexualization, but research is inconclusive. The behavioral indicators of sexualization may include flirting, seductiveness, increased masturbation, exhibitionism, sexual contact with older (or much younger) partners, or prostitution. These behaviors create obstacles to treatment because:

a. Crises are created that distract from the treatment.
b. Responsibility issues are clouded by the rationalization that the victim must have been "enjoying the sex" or that the victim seduced the offender in some way.
c. The victim becomes the negative focus of the family, frequently while the offender is "getting better."
d. The family's resistance increases as it finds ways to blame the problems on "the system."
e. Siblings revert to blaming the victim.
f. The victim may defend her- or himself by running away or by opposing reunification.

10. *Self-mastery and control.* The abused child does not have the same sense of choice and control over everyday life as the

healthy child. As a result, the abused child also lacks the advantages of learning from consequences because the logical connection between choice and consequence is not there. Despite the pseudomaturity and false sense of power, the child actually remains overly dependent and lacks the opportunity for responsible independence.

Chronology of Intervention Strategies for Ongoing Treatment

It is hoped that, by the end of the crisis intervention phase, much, if not most, of the legal process will have been completed. Although this eliminates some of the need for integration and teamwork, all it really does is to shift the focus to treatment planning and integration. Probably several counselors/therapists will be involved in the treatment process, especially if the whole family is involved. It is essential that there be close coordination among those involved. This certainly speaks to the advantage of having one coordinated treatment program, although treatment planning and integration are still workable in other situations.

1. *Peer support and therapy groups.* As soon as the crisis issues seem controlled, consideration should be given to group involvement. This may take the form of a play group at the younger ages to a peer support group in order to focus on social skills, interaction, appropriate development, and a supportive environment for expression of feelings and self-mastery. Some children may have a special need for group therapy to focus more intensively on feelings. This is a particularly good environment for dealing with issues of responsibility, anger, fear, and guilt. The presence of, and feedback from, peers can be tremendously validating and provide a continuing reality contact that may be more effective than one the adult counselor can provide. Peers also can be extremely validating of the treatment process. Of course, there's always the risk of the children expressing the negative experiences of treatment or "the system." Groups should be homogeneous in respect to age and, at the older end of this age group, in grouping by sex. Older children and adolescents can act as peer facilitators, with significant advantages to both the facilitator and the younger children. Groups should certainly be small enough to ensure appropriate control and supervision and allow time and space for expression (maximum of 6–8 children if there is supervisory help).

2. *Apology sessions.* If the family is moving in the direction of reunification, whether or not that actually happens, the major

events in this treatment phase may well be the apology sessions. If there is going to be no reunification, or if the contact was extrafamilial, modifications will have to be made to allow the victim psychologically to confront the offender. These sessions, whether direct or indirect in confrontation, will encourage venting, exploration of past patterns, and option-building for future patterns.

The apology sessions are a series of structured confrontations between the victim and offender and also may include the non-offending spouse and other family members. The first of these sessions may come early in the process, depending on the child's readiness, with the bulk of the sessions coming in the middle stage of treatment. The timing is flexible. The specific goals of these sessions will be apology, responsibility acceptance, report acceptance, and mutual commitment to treatment, regardless of chance of reunification. The offender also will accept responsibility for any consequences, such as incarceration.

Preparation for apology/confrontation session. The child must have a good sense of being protected before attempting an actual or psychological confrontation. This includes having been able to talk about the details of the abuse with the counselor and acknowledging the various feelings involved such as fear, rage, and guilt. Although these feelings don't yet need to have been resolved, they need to have been expressed and, as best as possible, understood. It should be clear to the child that the responsibility for the abuse rests with the offender and that there is a support system available (mother, counselor, school personnel, "the system") that believes her or him and will protect her or him from future harm. It is not necessary that the child "want" to see the father, although many children do at this point. It is important, however, that the child feel a sense of control over the timing and content of the session. The child can practice for the sessions through role-playing with the counselor or by writing letters or drawing pictures for the father (whether sent or not). The offender will have been similarly prepared.

The first session. The initial apology session should include the child, the offender, the spouse, the child's counselor, and the offender's counselor. The child should be the first to arrive, if possible, in order to meet the offender's counselor, see the room that will be used, and perhaps even arrange the chairs to be comfortable (children will frequently place themselves between their counselor and their mother). The child is reassured that any reactions, thoughts, or feelings will be permitted. The initial contact between child and offender may be anything from an icy lack of eye contact to a cheerful hug. The offender has to apologize for the abuse very specifically, as well as for other problems such as abusive language, physical abuse, or general disruption of the family. Responsibility issues will be clarified, and the report will be acknowledged as a positive and necessary action that will facilitate change in the family. Any reaction on the child's part will again be met with reassurance from all those present. The responses of any of the participants in the session are not often predictable. Details of the abuse may be given at this session or may be more appropriate at a future session.

Further sessions. The number and spacing of further apology sessions will be based on the judgment of the treatment team. The sessions will need to deal with the specific details of the abuse, so that minimization is avoided and all those in protecting roles have a clear picture. They will also have to address the setup used by the offender, including progressive patterns of seduction and substance use or abuse. The family should be aware of marital, communication, and parenting issues, although these may actually be addressed in more detail in future family sessions. One or more of the apology sessions should include all family members to ensure that the other children are aware of who is responsible for the abuse (they are quite likely to still blame the victim for causing all this difficulty), and to expose and break the "family secret" pattern. Special attention should be given to the siblings, who also have been victimized by fear, confusion, and stress within the family.

Indirect confrontation. The use of indirect confrontation may help either to prepare the child for a direct confrontation, process information from a direct session, or provide the child an opportunity for expression when a direct session is not possible (the offender is incarcerated, under a no-contact order, is extrafamilial, or even unknown). The same basic goals will apply: expressing feelings, clarifying responsibility, and creating protection. This can be facilitated through techniques like role-play with the counselor or with dolls, writing/dictating letters that may or may not be sent, drawing, or other expressive play (clay, paints, etc.).

The apology sessions are often the most challenging and rewarding for the counselor. They are frequently unpredictable, eliciting the whole spectrum of emotions from rage to tears. They are productive in that they may provide significant insight for both the family and counselors into the intra- and interpersonal dynamics and provide material for future individual and dyad sessions. The apology sessions also serve as important benchmarks when the treatment team makes decisions about visitation, and, eventually, possible reunification.

3. *Clarification of roles and responsibilities.* This stage of treatment involves both individual and family modalities. Specific strategies related to family systems will be addressed later when talking about family treatment. This may be a stage of long duration and overlap with earlier and later stages. Whereas the apology process focuses on the responsibility issues, this stage goes one step further to focus on the appropriate role of the child, a difficult task for the victim and family.

A major issue to tackle is the previously mentioned corporate family responsibility for the condition of the family system before, during, and after the abuse. Again, to emphasize, whereas the offender assumes 100% responsibility for the incident(s), the family also assumes its own responsibility. Acceptance of this responsibility is not easy for many families, and it is during this stage of treatment that major issues of resistance may arise. Having weathered the initial crises and, perhaps, the legal process, families are quick to see the problem as resolved and wish to forget the whole thing and put it behind them. This understandable but dangerous wish may cause the family to revert to the same dysfunctional patterns that existed prior to the abuse. It is also an easy trap for the counselor to embrace because the victim frequently will cooperate in this resistance. The family will rebel against the involvement of the "system" without any acknowledgment of their dependency needs and their lack of skills for independent healthy functioning.

Dealing with the victim individually during this phase also may mean focusing on resistance in the form of conflict over future roles and responsibilities. The child may well have significant difficulty in resuming appropriate child-level roles. The child may both enjoy and resent the pseudoadult power and the accompanying lack of real control. The counselor must set up the atmosphere for the child to be accepted as a child and set reasonable and appropriate limits for the child, in and out of the counselor's office.

The child can make most of the decisions regarding the activities/play during the sessions within a set of options that the counselor provides. Usually the child can bring a toy or game from home, or play with the toys in the counselor's office or playroom.

Like any other play therapy environment, the toys should be enjoyable and potentially expressive but also allow conversation and interaction with the counselor/therapist. Although expression of feelings is always an appropriate goal, during this phase there should also be an opportunity to set family roles and activities. The following techniques may be helpful.

    a. Family drawings are extremely useful on an ongoing basis to obtain a picture of past, current, or future structure. The drawings can be static or kinetic and are useful at different stages of treatment. Different components can be requested (child and siblings, child and parents, whole nuclear or extended family, pets, etc.).

    b. Small figures (dolls, play figures, clay) can represent the family or family members and can be moved to different structural or activity positions.

    c. The counselor can role-play situations, roles, or interactions either directly or through the use of dolls, stuffed animals, or puppets; for example, "Here's the big doll coming into the little doll's room. How does the little doll feel? What can he or she say?"

    d. Limits should be clear regarding behavior that is not acceptable in the sessions including hitting the counselor, self-harm, actual (as opposed to symbolic) destruction, and noise levels as determined by the setting.

    e. Limits should also be clear regarding physical and psychological space/distance in the room. The counselor should determine whether either arm's distance or lap-sitting feels comfortable and when hugs are OK.

    f. Roles can be clarified through appropriate responsibility. The parents can be encouraged to determine reasonable jobs or chores for the child to do and apply principles of encouragement and consequences to support doing these jobs. The counselor can reinforce the importance of these jobs to the child and discuss ways to do the jobs either more quickly or easily.

The victim needs to be able to return to the appropriate child role in the family, expressing feelings, receiving nurturance and protection, and taking on an age-appropriate share of responsibility within the family.

    4. *Empowerment.* This phase also overlaps with several others but empowerment is a primary issue at this, somewhat later, point in the treatment process. The empowerment process includes:

a. reinforcement of the report;
b. rebonding with the mother;
c. assertiveness and self-protection;
d. redefing the relationship with the father;
e. resumption of age-appropriate roles wherever possible; and
f. positive control and attitudes regarding sexuality.

One of the key elements in any form of sexual abuse is a power imbalance. Whether coercion, seduction, or force is used, the child is powerless against the physical, verbal, or affectional power tools of the adult. Victims may react in seemingly opposite ways. Whereas one child may assume the withdrawn, isolated, helpless stance, another may act out sexually, engage in aggressive activity, and rebel at school. Other children may react with pieces of other styles.

Regardless of the behavior, the root is the same: powerlessness and anxiety. These effects are sometimes doubly traumatic when one considers the family dynamics, where children often have been given unusually powerful, responsible, and pseudoadult roles before the abuse.

The child is likely to use inappropriate power techniques, then, in an attempt to regain some of the perceived lost power. The attempt, of course, backfires as the adults tend to either "fight fire with fire" or "give up," either pattern accelerating the power issues.

Parents can use typically suggested techniques for dealing with the power issues: set limits, clarify consequences, or withdraw from power struggles. They also, however, can use positive approaches to encourage appropriate empowerment, thereby reducing the child's need for unproductive power.

The first point in the recovery process for empowerment possibilities is the report. The report can be an extremely scary time for the child because it is such a powerful "weapon." It is necessary for protection and affects the rest of the family. The child needs strong reinforcement to view the report as a perfectly reasonable and appropriate step to "make things better" in order to stop dwelling on its devastating and traumatic aspects. Once the report has been made, the child should be reassured that the adults will take the responsibility for protecting the child.

Because the mother in a typical abuse case is torn between protecting her child(ren) and supporting her husband, her behavior is of critical importance to the child. The child should feel an immediate sense of protection from the mother, which can then progress to a "rebonding." The latter is emphasized by the mother-daughter dyad as the first to be brought into focus. This dyad will meet at various points throughout the treatment process to clarify and solidify the bond.

One of the most difficult goals of providing the child with a sense of empowerment is striking a balance between assertiveness and self-protection on one hand and aggressiveness and dictatorial power on the other. The child does have the capability for self-protection while maintaining the child role in the family. The basic message is similar to what we would give to an adult—taking care of oneself does not infringe on the rights of others or relieve one of social or familial responsibilities. This focus on assertiveness is facilitated greatly through the peer group work described earlier.

It seems obvious that the child's relationship with the father/offender must be redefined. Many in society would redefine the relationship by separating the two—by either incarcerating the offender or removing the child from the home. There are other options. Through the combination of individual, dyad, triad, and group treatment as well as carefully monitored visitation, a major shift in that relationship can be facilitated.

One frequent question lay and professional people often ask is how the victim or any of those involved can possibly "forgive and forget." The truth is that they don't. And they probably shouldn't. One analogy that may be helpful is that the abuse, like other traumatic events, is eventually "filed away"; that is, it certainly continues to exist as a memory but, with time, is integrated as part of experience and removed from everyday life. There may be times, of course, when the files are pulled back out so that some issues can be handled. This "filing" analogy allows victims and families to get on with their lives while still acknowledging the reality and responsibility. Although many variables may affect the child's ability to file things away, this method is clearly healthier than the denial and minimization that exemplifies the pathology.

The redefined relationship is accomplished by the father's assumption of an appropriate adult/parent/spouse role and the child's resumption of the child role. These roles are achieved through individual effort, including treatment, and the mutual support of the whole family.

The last focus in the empowerment phase is on positive attitudes and control regarding sexual issues. One of the typical rationalizations of the pedosexual offender is that he has provided sex education to the child. The problem, of course, is that the "education" provided is almost all negative, emphasizing exploitation over consensus, coercion over communication, and physical sensation over intimacy. The task of the treatment process, therefore, is to emphasize sex positivism—the concept that we can all maintain a positive attitude about our sexuality regardless of our experiences.

Sex positivism revolves around three principles (Rencken, 1986): knowledge, consensuality, and lack of harm. All three need to be addressed consistently during treatment. The child needs to receive *correct* and *complete* sexual information. This is sometimes resisted by the family who would almost like to psychologically "revirginize" the child and deny the sexualization. Information should include anatomy and physiology, human sexual responses (this can validate their own responses to the abuse), contraception, values, psychosexual development, relationships, and societal attitudes. Obviously, this information has to be set in an age-appropriate context.

The child also should receive strong messages about consensuality and lack of harm as contrasts to his or her own experience, and should receive balanced messages regarding self-protection and consensus, that being in positive control over self also includes a positive control over one's sexuality.

Empowerment, then, includes the concepts of positive, assertive control and responsibility. Positive control, in turn, goes along with appropriate power, both individually and in the family and society.

5. *Termination.* Although the duration of treatment may be highly variable, the child will probably be the first of the key people in the abuse situation to complete treatment. This, generally, has a lot to do with children's resilience and the normal healing process of development. If the treatment process involves the whole family, there is also the bonus that the child's progress can be monitored through longer duration modalities of marital and family contact. Readiness for termination can be assessed in four areas:

a. The child has successfully addressed all of the 10 treatment issues noted previously. They do not all need to be "resolved" perfectly, allowing for continuing healing. Particular emphasis should be placed on the empowerment and control issues because they will be necessary for further healing and protection.

b. The child is at minimal risk for revictimization, either by the original offender or another offender. I resolutely refuse to use the phrase "no risk" in referring to either victim or offender. Part of risk management lies in obtaining a strong commitment from the child to report new incidents or seek help from responsible adults who will believe and support the child. This may include building a solid adult support network. It also includes a firm agreement to return to the counselor for further sessions if there are any problems, whether or not they seem related to the abuse issues. The counselor may also wish to schedule phone contacts for the immediate future to cement that agreement.

c. The child has established a peer support system either through the treatment program or independently. The child is no longer isolated, although most children will not become outgoing or totally change their interactive styles.

d. The child has established and is maintaining an independent and age-appropriate life style. As termination approaches, the counselor will observe the child's increased ability to handle problems and decreased need to deal with them in treatment. The best treatment will have given the child the tools to be able to deal with these issues. Speaking of termination, Oaklander (1978) noted that "the child needs an opportunity to integrate, and assimilate with his own natural maturation and growth, the changes taking place as the result of the therapy." She adds, "Therapy begins to get in the way of his life." Another way of looking at this same issue is for the counselor to monitor her or his own reactions to the child. If the counselor is having more fun with the child during sessions rather than dealing with treatment issues, it is probably time to examine the possibility of termination.

As noted in the section on the young child, the termination session(s) should include some appropriate goodbye ritual including an exchange of small gifts, pictures, or drawings. There also should be a focus on the concept of the counselor "being there" and, certainly, a business card or other reminder of the counselor's address and phone number. Children frequently keep this in a "special place" for a long time after termination as a reminder of the support available.

Warning Signs and Cautions During Treatment

The counselor involved with a sexual abuse victim, whether as the primary therapist or team member, has a strong obligation to watch for warning signs. These may be signs of danger to the child or indicators of potential difficulties in the family or in the treatment process. The first of these dangers, of course, is the suicide risk discussed earlier. The counselor should be alert to severe depression, enduring guilt, and suicidal ideation such as "They would all be better off without me." Self-destructive tendencies can manifest as withdrawal or as high-risk behaviors. One 9-year-old stole a golf cart, drove it down a main street, and then crashed it into a riverbed.

Another major problem lies in the risk of victims dissociating. Although there is still much need for research (especially as this applies to children), it seems that dissociation in sexual abuse victims is likely to lead to the development of multiple personality disorders. Most of the adult survivors who do develop multiple personalities have not, apparently, had treatment as children, leading to some optimism. Particular attention should be paid to victims' statements that they "tuned out" during the sexual contact, or that they felt like they were somebody else watching the contact take place.

The rage factor, which is a very reasonable reaction and is present in most victims, also needs to be monitored. Although relatively rarely, rage can lead to a decompensation and psychotic reaction. Early emphasis on rage ventilation and reduction seems to be critical here.

Although the inappropriate power behavior mentioned earlier is to be expected, some children accelerate this behavior to the point of rejecting all authority in the family or society. Clearly, this rejection, frequently accompanied by resistance to therapy, leads to major problems in acting-out behaviors. The counselor consistently has to reinforce the advantages of positive control and responsibility without becoming another authority figure to the child. There may be occasions, however, where the counselor may need to be in the position of limit-setting.

The final caution for the counselor is to watch for black-and-white solutions or "pictures" that the child or the family paint. The very pathology that helped set up the abuse will lead to a "quick cure" if counselors go strictly by the child's or the family's reports. The counselor must remain strong and accountable throughout the process.

Victims of Other Pedosexual Behavior

Although most of the treatment process above applies to any victim of pedosexual contact with an adult, it focuses mostly on the intrafamilial setting with the regressed offender. Some added information will be helpful for dealing with other specific pedosexual situations.

The pedophile. Because the pedophile typically caters to the pleasure of the child, seducing the child with games, food, or other nurturing behavior, the victim is liable to express significant confusion. Victims may even be puzzled to learn that the pedophile is associated with harm. This is confounded by the fact that the victim may not have had anything to do with the report (because of multiple victims). Even after describing the pedophile's behavior, victims may, at most, acknowledge that *they* did something "dirty," not "good old Mr. Bob." Only after the involvement of police and, perhaps, an arrest, will many of the children acknowledge the seriousness of the problem and feel significant guilt or embarrassment. The responsibility issues should be clarified quickly. Because this form of contact is generally extrafamilial, there is a risk that treatment will not be mandated or monitored by child protective services. In addition, parents might hope that the problem will "blow over" and are not likely to risk embarrassment by initiating treatment voluntarily.

Another issue of concern for the victim of the pedophile is that probably other children who are known to the victim have been involved, either by concurrent or serial contact. The child will have to cope with the joint victimization and be reassured that *none* of the children were responsible for the behavior. The child may also have to be reassured that he or she can provide the names of other children involved because of the need for their protection, not because the child did something bad (i.e., the victim is not "tattling"). Because there is a strong probability that the pedophile will not admit to his behavior or its illegality, there is a likelihood that the victim will have to testify or, at least, give a taped statement or deposition. The child also may have to receive special attention if photographs, movies, or videotapes were taken. Because victims of pedophiles are more likely to be boys than victims of other forms of abuse, the section on the "male victim" should be consulted.

Rape. The rape victim consistently seems to be the most traumatized of the pedosexual victims in the following ways:

a. *Physical trauma.* Victims of rape experience more physical injury than any other victims of sexual abuse to the point that it is almost definitional. Serious physical injury (unless it is unrelated physical abuse) is almost always related to the violence of rape. The most common injuries, of course, are the result of actual or attempted forced penetration of the vagina or anus resulting in fissures, muscle tears, or internal damage from bruises to hemorrhage. Some damage can be permanent, particularly when it affects the female reproductive system.

b. *Emotional trauma.* The force, and threat of force, in the rape situation represents the ultimate coercion and creates the worst negative effects of coercion (Finkelhor, 1984). Trauma for the child is similar to that in adult rape victims, with two possible areas of increased vulnerability: the physical size/power differential is greater, leading to an even greater feeling of helplessness, and the child is less aware of the sexual context, focusing even more on the pain and violence of the situation. This is the area that generally will require the most intensive therapeutic intervention. If the offender is known to the victim, confrontation/apology sessions may be appropriate with careful preparation and planning.

c. *Need for long-term care.* The rape victim is likely to need lengthy treatment because of the high levels of physical and emotional trauma and also because of an inability to confront the offender. There is also the frustration that either the offender will not be caught or there may be the strain of trial testimony. There are likely to be very strong defensive mechanisms, including denial and dissociation, that may be resistant to treatment.

Sexual addiction/compulsion. The victim of this form of pedosexual contact is more likely to be an adoleslcent than a middle child, and is also more likely to be one of several "victims" as well as others affected by the offender. The victimization may occur either within or outside the family. Although there may well be a diffusion of energy or focus, the child still may experience the full range of emotions as do other pedosexual victims. The only mitigation is that the responsibility may more clearly rest on the offender, and it is more likely that the offender will be seen as "sick" or disordered. In communities with treatment programs geared specifically to this issue, the victim may be able to receive some additional support and, in some situations, benefit from some codependency exploration.

Symptomatic. The victim of the symptomatic offender may have different reactions depending on his or her closeness to the offender. One who is closely related, or has seen the offender for a long period of time, may be able to see the sexual contact as similar to other strange or bizarre symptoms and accept it as such but, at the age of 7 to puberty, even this view may be difficult and confusing. A victim to whom the offender is not known will face issues similar to those of other extrafamilial victims. Again, there may be some small benefit to knowing "the reason" for the contact, and some decrease in fear if it is seen as treatable.

The Male Victim

The specific plight of the male victim is one of the least understood in the whole arena of pedosexual behavior. Both the causes and effects of male victimization are less known than those of female victimization. As noted previously, the number and percentage of boy victims are probably significantly underreported compared to those of girls. This seems to be related to a societal belief that boys are not seen as "attractive" to adult men and that if there were any sexual contact, boys would "like it" and would not consider it abusive. The latter is a particularly feasible rationalization in the case of a female offender. As in female victimization, we are just now beginning to understand the male victim/female offender situation because we are probing adult men more intensively and "discovering" more cases. It seems that female offenders may more likely be aunts or babysitters rather than the father/stepfather position of male offenders.

At least at this point, in the reported cases that we do have, it is much more likely that the boy will be victimized by a male adult. Boys who are victimized also are more likely to be younger than girls, involved in extrafamilial settings, and be victimized in conjunction with other children (Finkelhor, 1984). This may be true in the pedophile situation or in other extrafamilial contacts (coaches, babysitters, youth leaders, and other trusted adults). This same-sex involvement is critical for the victim because sometime after the contact, and for some victims later than for others, there will be a concern about homosexuality. The male victim will question whether this has "made him" a homosexual or whether, in fact, he already was a homosexual and somehow set up the offense. This will be a factor, even though the offender may not have a preference for male adults. In fact, gay adults may have a lower incidence of same-sex contact with children than do heterosexual men, although research is needed here.

The male victim, therefore, even more than the female victim, will probably have more "why" questions: "Why me? Why a boy? Aren't you supposed to do that stuff to girls, not boys? Why pick a boy? Nothing fits anywhere. Why did I get hard? Why do the other kids call me queer when they did the same thing?" The answers are even more elusive.

We know very little about arousal patterns in same-sex pedosexual contact. Although there is some indication from offender reports of a history of sexual abuse, these data are incomplete and inconclusive. If there is a history of abuse, there may or may not be a connection between the age of the offender and the age of the new victim. We also have little information about behavioral specifics or duration of contacts.

The counselor should deal directly with homophobic concerns, even if the victim does not initiate discussion of the issue. The topic can be approached in a fairly routine way as a typical concern that children who have been put in this situation feel. Reassurance should certainly be given that this incident will not, in fact, cause homosexuality. The sex of the counselor may or may not be significant depending on the child's needs; however, male counselors may have to pay extra attention to both the possible homophobic concerns and the importance of male role modeling. The boy will need to receive strong messages that validate warmth and sensitive nurturing as well as strength and power.

The middle child provides a complex series of challenges for the counselor who is either in the primary or supportive role. For most children, prognosis can be optimistic, with the natural healing process working in a positive, parallel track with treatment. This should not, however, in any way call the need for treatment into question. Sexual abuse does not get better on its own, either while the behavior is occurring or during the healing and recovery process. It also does not get better without the active support and involvement of parents, whether the abuse occurred within or outside the home. The child has a right to treatment and recovery.

The Adolescent

Adolescents differ in several important ways from the previously discussed age groups, both in terms of issues and in terms of intervention strategies. One major difference is that the adolescent is more likely to be a "survivor" as well as a victim. In other words, the pedosexual behavior may have happened a significant time before the counselor encounters this troubled client. For the purpose of this book, we will define an immediate intervention as one that occurs within one year of the last pedosexual contact, and a delayed intervention as one that occurs after a year. There even may be some benefit in defining an even longer delayed intervention, but that raises more questions than it answers.

Up to this point we have used the term "victim" in alluding to children. This has been an intentional emphasis on the child's total lack of responsibility for the contact, and also on the child's helplessness within the situation. Several of the treatment issues and goals previously noted address the movement away from that helplessness to a feeling of appropriate power and control. It could certainly be said that the treatment process helps to move the child from the "victim" role to the "survivor" role. Many victims, of course, become survivors even without treatment, although, perhaps, with more difficulty or less efficiency. The adolescent in need of delayed intervention is presumably one of the survivors who is having difficulty with that process. The survivor, of course, deserves significant positive "strokes" for coping as well as he or she has done in the survival process so far, but the survivor still may be experiencing significant pain and suffering. In this section, we will identify differences, when they exist, between immediate (victim) and delayed (survivor) intervention. We also may refer to the "victim/survivor" as an inclusive category.

How do adolescents differ from the previous age groups in terms of normal developmental issues? The major issues revolve around the establishment of identity and independence, clearly evolving a sense of self as opposed to family (Salkind & Ambron, 1987).

Erikson (1968) identified the task of this age group as "identity versus role diffusion." Obviously, this normal task will be of interest to us in looking at the adolescent victim/survivor with the inherent and considerable role confusion. Elkind (1967) also talked of an adolescent egocentrism where adolescents become self-absorbed and self-conscious, acknowledging others' thoughts and opinions, but imagining these thoughts to be centered on them, the adolescents. We, as a society, certainly reinforce this sense by assigning a great value to the fashions, life style, and spirit of the adolescent, with many adults maintaining an adolescent outlook, including a significant egocentrism and lack of responsibility. A great value is placed on adolescent independence and rebellion (witness the large number of movie plots based on teenage themes that could be subtitled, "Teen knows best" or "Adults really are hopeless geeks").

How do these developmental issues differentiate adolescents from the middle child previously discussed? How do adolescent issues evoke concerns regarding pedosexual contact? There is, perhaps most significantly, a normal increase in sexual behavior, both because of the issues of independence and identity and because of the onset of puberty. Although much of this sexual behavior is self-directed and controlled, it also is clearly affected by peer involvement. "Normal" sexual expression is a perfect "vehicle" for the sexualized adolescent in that sex can be accepted and can be a useful tool for survival, coping, and controlling a scary situation. Having learned that sexual feelings can be exploited and used in a highly controlling fashion, the adolescent victim/survivor can obtain physical pleasure, attention, affection, peer acceptance, and even financial independence through the use of sex.

Conversely, a different set of victim/survivors goes into adolescence with an abhorrence and fear of sex, withdrawing from peers and the typical adolescent adjustment needs perhaps with a pseudomature "I don't need them" attitude. These extremes of the highly controlling and the highly controlled are typical of sexualized adolescents and set them off from the more general postpubertal sexual behavior. In both cases, there also, of course, may be considerable difficulty in establishing any real intimacy patterns. The exaggeration of control and intimacy dysfunctions of abuse survivors is, unfortunately, overrepresented among prostitutes, nude dancers and models, and in sexually explicit media.

Another major difference that should be a concern for counselors is that the adolescent, when compared to the young child or the middle child, is much more likely to attempt suicide and more likely to succeed in the attempt. Although we are still gathering helpful research data regarding adolescent suicide, it seems clear that the desperation, powerlessness, and hopelessness of the abuse victim dramatically increases the risk of both attempting and succeeding at suicide. Two studies make this connection effectively. Kosky (1983) reported that suicidal behavior was associated with losses, underachievement, divorce, or other marital disputes among the parents, and abuse of the child. McKenry, Fishler, and Kelly (1982) reported that factors such as "family conflict, family cohesion, and parental behavior" were critical. Clearly, both of these studies would point toward the abused (particularly the sexually abused child) as being at risk. Male victims may be at even higher risk.

The increased independence of the adolescent age group leads to two major concerns for counselors. One is that there is a significant resistance to treatment because there is not, necessarily, a strong motivation to reunite with the family and, specifically, to have any contact with the offender. The teenager may well rather move out than have further contact as a result of the sexualization and the pseudomaturation (this can also be a power play). The second, related, concern is that there is a clear risk of runaway behavior. This may take the form of a relatively typical overnight runaway, or it may be of significant duration. Again, this may be a power play, but the sexualized child is more likely to have a strong motivation for independence. Interestingly, one of the factors that may keep this child in the family is her or his concern for the risk of younger siblings being abused.

Peer relationships are typically critical for the adolescent, with acceptance as the minimal criterion and leadership as an ideal for many. Ideally, there would be a balance between sexes in these relationships (some same-sex, some opposite). As noted in the discussion of sexual behavior, the abuse victim is more likely to swing more radically between the extremes of peer relationships, from withdrawal and isolation to a strong need for acceptance. Both of these extremes tend to minimize the possibility of a strong, appropriate peer support system. The same behavior (e.g., sexual relations) that the victim uses to try to gain acceptance frequently backfires when the peer group labels her as "easy" or a "boy-stealer."

The adolescent also runs a higher risk of developing severe reactions that may not typically surface until adulthood, particularly if there has been no treatment. These include dissociative reactions and various eating and other self-concept disorders, from anorexia to obesity. The counselor must be on guard to these issues.

All of these typical adolescent developmental concerns simply become magnified for the abuse victim/survivor. Even the brightest, most insightful adolescent will have significant difficulty with these issues.

The Report

In either immediate or delayed intervention, the adolescent may be more concerned about confidentiality than younger children are. Although this may cause some difficulty during the report timeframe, it should not deter the counselor from making the report. The adolescent may be less vulnerable and better able at self-protection than the younger child, but still needs the protection that is generally mandated.

Possibly more important that the sense of protection is the sense of validation that comes from the report. This may be true at all age levels but is particularly important for the adolescent. Even if there are objections from the child or the parents, the report is an indication that the child is worth "the trouble" and worth the caring of the person who makes it. There also, of course, may be younger siblings at risk.

The adolescent may well see the system as unbelieving or nonsupportive during the investigation and may question the worth of the report, so an extra measure of support at this time is necessary. Much more than the other age groups, the adolescent may be blamed, at least partially, for the sexual contact. The abuse may even play out a heavily reinforced male fantasy. If the abuse is ongoing or was still occurring not too long before the report, there is also a good chance that it is a contact of long duration that began in preadolescence. There are relatively few pedosexual relationships that are initiated in adolescence (Finkelhor, 1984).

The delayed intervention presents unique problems with the report. The counselor feels a dilemma in reporting a pedosexual contact that last happened 3, 4, or even 10 years ago. There generally is no "statute of limitations" involved in mandatory reporting laws, whereas there may be a limit (either statutory or practical) for prosecuting the offender. Theoretically, the counselor could be cited for failing to report a crime that could not be prosecuted. This would be extremely unlikely, however, and the counselor would be well advised to talk with the local CPS authorities to determine particular plans. This is another good argument in favor of close teamwork with CPS, who could be cooperative in determining risk as well as the need for a formal report or investigation.

Crisis Intervention

The crisis stage for an adolescent may be more difficult to deal with, again because of the increased risk of suicide or runaway behavior. The counselor may have to do a considerable amount of general stabilizing before dealing with the abuse issues. Trust-building must be a major initial focus.

Any counselor who works with adolescents knows about trust-building. The skilled counselor masters the ability to gain both trust and respect while maintaining an appropriate adult role and an appropriate distance. The adolescent has a difficult time trusting an adult who is either too close or too distant. This normal concern is magnified by the pedosexual contact.

Sexual abuse strikes at the heart of the ability to trust. Whether or not the contact was initiated at a younger age, the adolescent victim is more likely to have kept the secret (despite phsycial and emotional pain) for a longer period of time than a younger child would have, with an almost constant feeling of betrayal along with the love-hate ambivalence discussed earlier. Even more so at this age, the victim is also likely to feel a lack of trust and significant rage toward the mother and consider her a coconspirator because she failed to protect. These feelings sometimes may be stronger when directed at the mother than when directed at the offender.

Once these feelings are understood, it is easier to see the mistake that many counselors (of either sex) make—that of trying to act like a mother to the "poor baby" victim/survivor. This counselor reaction is much closer to pity than empathy and may include uninvited physical contact (hugs, hand-holding), loss of affective control (crying, anger), and verbal revictimization ("poor kid, it must have been horrible, how disgusting that must have felt"). In looking back on this time period, one insightful survivor commented that the worst thing was what she called "the big lie" when adults say "I understand." The counselor must remain strong but not controlling, available but not intrusive, and honest in stating that he or she does *not* understand but would like to be a supportive and caring listener.

Counselors also are cautioned not to engage in "offender-bashing." As mentioned, it is easy for adults to identify with the rage the victim feels but less easy to identify with a victim's ambivalence. Consider the following interchange:

> Client: I just hate him! My skin crawls when I think of him touching me. I wish he would die!
> Counselor: He sounds like a real son of a bitch. What a creep!
> Client: Well, he didn't used to be. It was only when he was drinking.

The client quickly became defensive about the counselor's name-calling for two reasons: it pushed the ambivalence button and it took the focus away from the client's feelings. A more helpful reflection would have been, "You sound really angry." The victim's feelings should be the focus for support even when they shift or seem unclear.

Like the young child's, the adolescent's trust is formed by the counselor's "being there." If at all possible, the same person should remain as the primary therapist for the duration of treatment. The adolescent may frequently test the counselor's limits and willingness to "be there" by calling the counselor between appointments, setting up phone calls between counselor and teacher or parents, or trying to "shock" the counselor with smoking, drinking, or sexual behavior or language.

The concept of "being there" is critical to a *treatment contract* that can be a useful option during this phase. Although part of this contract will act as an anti-suicide and running away contract, it will also serve as a more general, long-term agreement. It should be created anew in each case and remain flexible enough to be renegotiable as treatment progresses. It should emphasize counselor availability as well as the client's commitment to attend sessions and to call the counselor before taking impulsive action. It should also clarify the limits of confidentiality regarding what will be shared with parents, CPS, lawyers, and others. Adolescents will generally like the adult feeling of entering into a contract. Most importantly, the contract will act as an additional, concrete bond in the trust process.

The final issue of the trust process is the child's perception of the counselor's role as it relates to both "the system" and to parents. This goes beyond the confidentiality issue to the issue of "For whom does the counselor work"? The adolescent will have more difficulty with trust if the counselor seems to be an extension of "the system" or of parents—that the counselor is another authority figure who is trying to "get" the child to "behave," force her or him home, and either push reunification or split the family. Conversely, the trust level will improve if the adolescent sees the counselor as an advocate within the system. Ideally, there is an added bonus if the child perceives that the entire treatment team is working and advocating for him or her, but this may be difficult for the child to see, especially during the time of crisis.

As noted, the major issue to be stabilized during the crisis phase is the risk of suicide or runaway behavior. Trust-building is the initial step in accomplishing this, including use of the contract. It is important for the counselor to move quickly to clarify responsibility, which will be an ongoing task. In this phase, the adolescent not only has to recognize the offender's sole responsibility for the abuse but also clearly accept the responsibility for his or her own recovery. The focus can be positive and centered around "here-and-now" issues as well as future planning. Even during discussion of the facts and feelings around the abuse, the focus can still be on how this history can be brought under control now. This is sometimes more difficult for the adolescent than for younger children because adolescents typically have a clearer memory of the painful details. This positive here-and-now focus assists the adolescent to feel in control and avoid the feeling of alienation that leads to both of the high-risk behaviors mentioned above. Alienation is significantly worsened if mother does not believe the child, highlighting feelings of rejection.

The adolescent is less likely to experience the fears typical of the younger age groups. There is, however, a more subtle but pervasive sense of wondering "What's going to happen to me?" Although the adolescents' egocentrism helps to fuel a veneer of confidence, there is considerable anxiety over rejection before the self-identity is completely formed. It's the kind of doubt that even good bakers experience—the bread has risen, the crust looks brown, but how do we know if it's done inside (and there's some concern about the reliability of the oven!)? The counselor has to address this concern of rejection by reassuring the adolescent that she or he will be involved in planning options and that even these options can be revised based on her or his comfort level.

The final general concern during the crisis phase (both in immediate and delayed intervention) is the issue of victim veracity. As noted in the earlier sections, the adolescent is *more* likely than a younger child (although the number is probably still low) to make a false allegation intentionally. Clearly, improved cognitive and verbal ability increases that possibility; however, the adolescent is also more likely to understand the consequences (separation from family, trial, incarceration, general family chaos). There are, certainly, some extremely dysfunctional situations where the child may accept these consequences as an alternative to an abusive or unstable situation. Unless the child is seen as psychotic or severely antisocial, there is probably some severe problem if an allegation is made even if this sexual abuse allegation is not true. A plan for protection may still be needed independently of decisions regarding prosecution of the offender. There also may be a need for a protection plan if the child recants the allegation, whether or not it was true!

Some unique issues pertain in the delayed crisis intervention. The first of these, at the risk of being obvious, is to acknowledge the crisis. It would be possible to think that because time had elapsed since the last incident, there would be no crisis. There are two major sources of crisis: divulging the abuse, and the precipitating problem (which may initially seem to be unrelated).

Like adult survivors, the adolescent may divulge the abuse only after establishing a trusting relationship. Although this may occur with peers or family, the counseling relationship provides the atmosphere for most delayed reports. The presenting problem(s) may be relationship difficulties (boyfriend, sex, jealousy, pregnancy, rejection), school problems (academic, social, attention, homework, acting-out behavior), substance abuse, or issues of self-worth (depression, eating disorders, running away). These problems, in and of themselves, may be at the crisis level.

Divulging the abuse usually will precipitate a crisis because it represents such a departure from "the secret" and will be upsetting, at some level, to the status quo, both intrapsychically as well as in the family system. This crisis may be met by minimization, rationalization, and denial from significant others (more so than in immediate intervention), and legal intervention is less likely to occur or to be effective.

The adolescent, then, may need considerable support in divulging the abuse. The counselor will have to create an atmosphere of trust and "ask the right questions." Many otherwise good counselors report hearing of only a few sexual abuse cases because they simply do not ask about it. This is particularly true in the delayed intervention. The "right questions" are actually permission statements rather than interrogatives—"it's OK to talk about what happened in your family; sometimes feelings like yours are connected to stuff that happened in the past; it sounds like you've been keeping some sort of secret for a long time."

As with younger children, the counselor would first focus on the survivor's feelings rather than on the details of the pedosexual behavior. This should certainly remain as the primary focus, but the delayed intervention presents an exceptional situation in that the details may not be investigated or otherwise addressed. The counselor again will give permission for the details to be discussed (rather than interrogating) and should also give permission for the details to be disclosed at intervals over time, allowing the picture to form as slowly as necessary.

Decisions will have to be made whether direct or indirect confrontation with the offender is appropriate. Even though the "apology session" technique will be discussed in the next treatment phase, decisions regarding that structure will need to be made earlier in the crisis phase in the case of a delayed intervention.

The crisis intervention phase of treatment is particularly critical in delayed intervention. There is a good chance of panic on the part of the adolescent once the abuse is divulged. The counselor almost may have to approach the child with an attitude that each session may be the last intervention before the child leaves home, drops out of school, or the family moves, until the situation is stabilized. The counselor may well have to "buy time" and offer as much support as possible.

Ongoing Treatment

We will again review Sgroi's list of 10 treatment issues and relate them to the adolescent age group (Porter, Blick, & Sgroi, 1982). These apply to both immediate and delayed intervention.

1. *"Damaged goods" syndrome*. Adolescents will be more concerned than younger children about the physical effects of sexual abuse including pregnancy, sexually transmitted diseases, and hymen damage (even though the latter is also of concern to many nonsexualized children). These concerns can either be related directly to the abuse or be indirectly related to sexualization. Adolescents also become aware that they may not be able to "save themselves" for a special first-time sexual experience. Clearly, sensitive medical intervention with counseling support is essential, even when there is no "major" physical trauma.

2. *Guilt*. The adolescent may not only feel responsible for the pedosexual contact, like the middle child, but also may feel responsible for any sexual or behavioral acting-out that has occurred. The counselor can assist the adolescent to assume responsibility and control over current behavior without feeling guilty for the sexualization. The adolescent may also feel guilty for not actively stopping the abuse at an earlier time, especially if the abuse was of long duration.

3. *Fear*. The fear issues, specifically the fear of alienation, have been noted previously. In ongoing treatment, the fear of alienation is closely related to trust of the counselor, peers, and, most of all, family. The adolescent may also fear retaliation, either in the form of physical threat or in the form of rejection and alienation from the family.

4. *Depression*. Ongoing depression and recurring suicidal ideation should be anticipated. The counselor should renew the suicide contract periodically.

5. *Low self-esteem and poor social skills*. Adolescents typically have concerns about self-esteem. These are greatly magnified in the victim/survivor, particularly as they relate to body image and a sense of general unworthiness. These image problems may manifest themselves specifically in various eating disorders. Although

obesity may be observed and relatively easily monitored by the counselor, anorexia and bulimia may have less visible but disastrous effects. The counselor will have to monitor eating patterns directly with the child and with the family. Although eating disorders are associated more often with female victims, male victims also have significant body image issues and may compulsively participate in athletic or bodybuilding activities, or *totally* avoid them!

6. *Repressed anger and hostility.* Although more adolescents than younger children are able to express their anger and rage directly, many continue to repress or deny those feelings. Defenses include withdrawal, minimization, passive-aggressive behavior, histrionics, and dissociation. The latter is a significant concern for counselors because the victim/suvivor is in an extremely vulnerable position. Many adolescent victims show at least some dissociative behaviors that may be relatively subtle and could slip by unless carefully monitored.

7. *Inability to trust.* As noted, trust and alienation issues are particularly important for the adolescent and are magnified for the sexual abuse victim.

8. *Blurred role boundaries and role confusion.* Role boundary problems are usually set before adolescence and that system is difficult to modify, thus it may cause major stress for the adolescent. If the role confusion has persisted, the victim will be understandably reluctant to give up the power of an inappropriate role, even if the power has been anxiety-provoking.

9. *Pseudomaturity and failure to complete developmental tasks.* Not only is the loss of power significant, but there is also a sense of lost childhood. A frequently expressed part of the rage is the grief over lost or denied childhood experiences—"I should have been playing with dolls instead of his penis." The loss of peer experiences may also be important because victims feel isolated from age-mates and gravitate toward older friends.

10. *Self-mastery and control.* These issues will be expanded upon in the discussion of empowerment. The adolescent needs to take responsibility for the recovery process and become accountable for current behavior in order to gain a sense of control.

Treatment Strategies

Treatment strategies will be reviewed chronologically with an emphasis on adolescent issues.

Apology session(s). There are two unique issues for the adolescent in the apology process: resistance to the session and increased probability of rage reactions.

The older the child, the more likely the child is to exhibit significant resistance to apology sessions. This resistance may take the form of "I never want to see that slime again," or "It's no big deal, it's over, why do we need the hassle?" This polarity of rage and passive-aggressive behavior is evident not only among different victims but also within one victim at different times. This resistance may be strong and of long duration, probably becoming even stronger as time passes without a confrontation. Although the victim's comfort level and readiness should certainly be considered, there may be a point at which the counselor may actively encourage or even push for the apology sessions. The sessions, even if there is only one, may be extremely valuable in exploring the resistance, ventilating feelings, and clarifying responsibility and may result in a significant therapeutic breakthrough. Allowing the child to control totally the therapy process through resistance may reinforce the pseudomaturity, power issues, and dependence on rigidity for control.

The other unique issue for adolescents in the apology process is the intensity of rage they may express during the apology session(s). Because of adolescents' verbal ability and the duration of the emotional repression, their rage can be strong and needs to be handled carefully by the counselor, balancing expression with control. In one apology session, I heard a 15-year-old girl string together 20-minutes worth of nonstop epithets, expletives, and anger in rather creative combinations. Fortunately, the offender was prepared and willing to listen, and the result was a clear therapeutic success. The girl was able to see the offender taking responsibility, acknowledging her feelings, and maintaining self-control.

The delayed intervention also has its own set of issues. The counselor, in consultation with the treatment team, when available, will have to determine whether the victim should confront the offender directly or indirectly. Factors in this decision include the victim's current relationship and contact with the offender, extent and duration of the abuse, possible risk to the offender (rejection, retaliation), and whether or not a formal report has been made.

If a direct confrontation is planned, both offender and survivor should be prepared in advance, even if this means that the offender might refuse to cooperate (it's better to know that in advance). Ideally, both should also commit to several sessions (at least 3) to work through the various issues. The direct confrontation generally can have the same goals as other apology sessions discussed earlier, but with the added goal of dealing with "the secret."

Indirect confrontation can be much the same as in the case of the younger child except, again, for the possibility of greater resistance or rage.

Group strategies. After the immediate crisis intervention issues have been addressed and, perhaps, concurrently with the apology sessions, the adolescent can gain greatly from participating in a group. At least two types of groups should be considered: therapy and support.

The therapy group ideally should be led (or cofacilitated) by a counselor other than the primary therapist to provide a different perspective and further validation of the issues and the ability of the victim to deal with them. This group would have similar goals to those of individual therapy, with a special focus on validation. This validation includes reassurance about the report, support for the feelings of ambivalence as well as rage, and shared perceptions ("I'm not the only one in the world who felt like _____"). The group can help clarify roles and responsibilities, deal with empowerment, and greatly reduce the risk of alienation. Most successful groups are fairly homogeneous in age; developmental issues as well as the desirability of same-sex or coed groups also need to be considered when forming groups.

The therapy group should be available from 6 to 12 months and then can be followed by a support group. The support group will continue the validation and empowerment process, including assertiveness and sex education. The support group can also deal with more "typical" adolescent concerns—relationships, school, career—and how these concerns may or may not be affected by the abuse. An additional therapy-oriented group may be useful for some adolescents to return to during, or after, the support group.

Clarifying roles and responsibilities. This phase of treatment takes some of the results of the apology session and refines the roles and responsibilities within the family. As noted earlier, the adolescent may be well entrenched and enmeshed in a "parentified" role, a powerful position that has provided some of the few "positives" in life. It is more difficult at this age, of course, to give the permission message to *be* a child. In effect, that process at this age would mean to *return to being* a child, a role that some victims have never learned.

There are some messages that can be helpful to the adolescent:

- It is not necessary to act like an adult in order to be accepted/appreciated/acknowledged.
- It's OK to have fun.
- Adolescents *do* have responsibilities but they are not the same as adults'.
- Peers can understand and relate as friends.
- Time can be used as a part of the healing process and to avoid impulsive decisions.

During this phase it will be important not only to acknowledge the responsibility of the offender, as previously discussed, but also the role of the mother (or nonoffending spouse). The adolescent frequently shows what seems to be an inordinate amount of rage toward the mother for not protecting. The rebonding process begins in this phase with the clarification of what roles mother *and* child have been assuming. At this time, mother may well acknowledge feelings of guilt, sadness, and jealousy. Depending on the maturity and emotional stability of the mother, she may see the adolescent as a "rival" at this point, which might further support her "choice" of the offender. These feelings may become so overwhelming that mother may detach herself from the victim as a coping mechanism. The counselor should be aware of this possibility and provide additional support during this early part of the rebonding process.

One of the major concerns in this phase is familial resistance to treatment and a reoccurrence of "blaming the victim." This is a special problem in adolescence because the family is more likely to see the victim as enjoying the contact ("otherwise she's big enough to have said no") and less in need of support ("if she/he doesn't like it around here, they can leave"). Normal and magnified adolescent limit-testing will tend to aggravate this process. Combined with the "hassles" the family has experienced with the CPS and legal system, there is a high risk at this point that mother will, intentionally or not, "choose" the offender over the victim and either agree to an out-of-home placement or force a runaway situation.

Empowerment. As noted, both group and individual modalities should be used for the adolescent empowerment process. The same sequence is applicable: report reinforcement, rebonding, assertiveness, redefining paternal relationships, age-appropriate roles, and positive controls and attitudes about sexuality. Two of these should be expanded as they pertain to the adolescent.

The process of rebonding with the mother is frequently more complicated and fragile in this age range. There is a clear risk of rejection and alienation and difficulty in defining a relationship that is different from one that had existed for a long time. There may be significant positives in looking at common issues and concerns *outside* of the family and its history to balance the strong focus on the abuse. Examples of these include: women's issues in society, career options, school planning and options, and peer relationships. This focus may actually encourage the opening of communication so that feelings about the abuse may be discussed more reasonably.

The second important focus in this age group is on the positive control and attitudes regarding sexuality. Because sexual behavior is likely to occur in this age group normally, the adolescent victim/survivor is likely to be (or have been) involved with problematic sexual contact such as much older partners, high frequency behavior, sexually transmitted diseases, or pregnancy. The ultimate problem may be a dramatically increased exposure to and risk of contracting AIDS, although the research has not *yet* shown the effects.

The clear focus, again in both individual and group modalities, needs to be on gaining control of the sexual behavior rather than using sexual behavior to fulfill needs for acceptance and affection. This probably does not call for a "just say no" approach. Rather, the question becomes, "How can you feel more in control of the sexual situation?" This may include reducing the number of partners, intentional discussions with partners, use of contraceptives and safety barriers, masturbation (both as a "substitute" and a discovery technique for positive feelings), and, of course, accurate information about sex.

A closely related issue is body image. Much of sexual behavior may be related to "proving" attractiveness and desirability with little real pleasure (anorgasmia may be typical). Victims/survivors may use excessive makeup (or none at all) and dress provocatively (or plainly) and use starvation (or binging) as ways to cope with a negative body image. Part of the empowerment process can consist of receiving information and support for nutrition, exercise, and self-care as well as smoking, alcohol, and other addictive or self-destructive substances.

There also may be same-sex exploration during this age range. Although this may be normal, the counselor should reinforce the issue of positive choice and control to ensure that this is not exclusively a reaction to the abuse. Homosexual issues for the male victim will be addressed later.

Another effective strategy for empowerment is the use of stabilized adolescent survivors as peer facilitators for group therapy/ support and as "sponsors" for other victims in earlier phases of treatment. This can be clearly helpful for both "sides" of the contact. This strategy can greatly improve the sense of control and accomplishment of the survivor, clarify issues, and provide role modeling.

Termination. Unfortunately, in this treatment phase, there may not be a clear or typical termination. Due to either positive or negative effects, the adolescent's independence is likely to lead to a client-initiated termination, perhaps before the counselor had planned. This typically takes the form of client no-shows and cancellations. Once the counselor sees this pattern, an attempt should be made to schedule a termination session in order to obtain closure.

Like the younger age groups, the adolescent should be able to demonstrate self-protection, including the willingness to seek help from family, counselors, or the authorities.

Warning Signs and Risks

As noted in the crisis intervention phase, the risk of suicide remains real throughout the treatment process. The counselor needs to be aware of statements of depression, helplessness, hopelessness, and alienation from family or peers. Renegotiation of the suicide contract can validate the client's importance to the counselor and can be done from a positive perspective, emphasizing the areas where the client had gained control or made progress.

Runaway behavior also remains an ongoing risk. This could be either solitary or accompanied, with a friend of either the same or opposite sex. Again, a contract is helpful with, at least, an agreement to contact the counselor for reassurance of safety.

The risk of dissociative behavior is more of a factor for the adolescent than for younger children. Although this is usually caught early in the process, the counselor should still be alert to statements or behaviors that indicate a "tuning out" or a feeling of being a spectator to the abuse or other behavior, particularly in sexual relationships. This process may be part of the reported lack of pleasure that many survivors report.

Other Forms of Pedosexual Contact

Specific issues related to adolescents will be briefly addressed here.

Pedophilia. Although pedophilia, by definition, applies only to prepubertal children, we have included the two forms of adolescent preference, hebephilia and ephebophilia, under this category in the taxonomy. Both of these forms may be closer in their dynamics to adult preference than is pedophilia (see chapter 3). Hebephilia may be a variant of heterosexual adult preference with an emphasis on the emerging development, "innocence," powerlessness, or fixation based on inadequacy. Likewise, in male offenders, ephebophilia may be a variant of homosexual adult preference with similar emphases.

The adolescent victim/survivor could, of course, have been victimized by a pedophile at a younger age and may feel uncomfortable/ambivalent about making a report versus keeping the secret. There may even be a lingering feeling of rejection if the pedophile had not kept various promises to the victim or if the pedophile had moved on to yet a younger child.

The victims of the hebephile/ephebophile may primarily feel exploited. They may have thought of the offender as a good friend, different from other adults. They may also have felt loved in an adult sense for the first time, and, therefore, validated for their own attractiveness and maturity. When they discover that this validation was only for sexual purposes, they may totally reverse this validation and see themselves as "damaged goods," unattractive, and incompetent. Clearly, trust will be a major issue for these victims.

Rape. Like adult rape victims, the adolescent victim feels both the trauma of the rape and the "victim-blaming" syndrome. Adolescents are susceptible to being castigated for short skirts, shorts, makeup, or other "seductive" behaviors regardless of the irrelevance of these to the rape dynamics.

As discussed earlier, the rape victim will have to deal with both physical and emotional trauma, including the probability of magnified reactions to the "damaged goods" syndrome and to the rage factor, including a strong possibility of "anti-male" feelings. Dissociation and gender dysphoria are both clear risks.

Addictive and symptomatic. Although younger children may gain some solace in realizing that these offenders are in some way "sick," the adolescent may feel increased ambivalence because of the same factor. There is a sense that "I should have known that there was something wrong with him" or "How could I have let *him*?" The counselor may need to attend to the responsibility issues at some length.

The Male Victim

The adolescent male victim will have different reactions depending on the sex of the offender. Although research is clear that most offenders are male (Finkelhor, 1984), it is not clear whether there may be different dynamics affecting this age group that research has not identified because of the very effects of the problem. This is not to say that male offenders are in the minority but rather that there may be more "unreported" female offenders.

The female offender may see the male adolescent as a rejuvenating experience, particularly under the influence of alcohol or other drugs. The male victim, having been programmed by movies (e.g., "The Graduate") or sexually explicit media, may see this as a male fantasy come true. Although there may be some clear discomfort, particularly the closer the offender is to the victim, (e.g., stepmother or aunt), the male adolescent is likely to see this as a positive experience. Clinical experience verifies that adults looking back on such contacts do not see them as abusive or describe them as molestations. How much of an impact such contacts generally have—positive, negative, or neutral—is simply not clear and should be explored thoroughly in each case.

The effect is much more clear and dramatic in the case of a male offender. Whether the contact happened during middle childhood and was not reported until adolescence, or if it happened more recently, the male victim/survivor will probably have a strong homophobic reaction. He will have strong concerns that either he was already homosexual prior to the abuse or has become homosexual as a result. This feeling is much stronger in adolescence and seems to occur even if heterosexual peer contact has already taken place. It is not clear whether, beyond this homophobia, there may be deeper sex-identity confusion because adolescence is a critical period for the establishment of identity. At any rate, the counselor will have to be extremely sensitive to these issues.

The Youthful Offender

The minor offender has become a topic of considerable interest, presumably as an offshoot of the general interest in pedosexual behavior. Although most of these offenders are adolescents (thus, the discussion at this point), some are prepubertal.

One of the tricky parts of this issue is in determining the difference between "sex play" and an "offense." Although some people would argue that all pedosexual contact is offensive, much of this contact is developmentally normal, especially between/among peers. The major variable that makes the contact abusive is a force/coercion/power factor that has not adequately been defined by research. We have arbitrarily established a 5-year age difference (Finkelhor, 1984) to indicate a significant difference in power that would therefore define abuse. Although this is helpful, it defines only part of the abuse equation and does not deal with the "coercion" issue that the same author considers important. Clearly, children and adolescents can be coercive with another child or adolescent who is less than 5 years younger. This coercion can be physical or verbal, the latter being important for children who have been sexualized and have some "knowledge" advantage.

The issue of sexualization leads to the discussion of the offender-as-victim-as-offender. Although exact numbers are unclear, evidently a majority of youthful offenders have been victims themselves although, perhaps, untreated. Although the effect of sexualization is the biggest factor here, the dynamics of the victim of abuse are similar to those of the offender in this age group—isolation, alienation, and a lack of intimacy. The sexualization acts as the magnifying glass, focusing these dynamics into a pedosexual contact.

How does a victim turn into an offender? Clinical observations may provide helpful information. The pedosexual behavior is likely to be limited to genital touching, although there may be other sexual behavior such as exhibitionism or voyeurism. The victim is likely to be prepubescent and known to the offender, whether intra- or extrafamilial. The youthful offender is likely to have a history of physical or emotional abuse in addition to sexual victimization. This may reflect a generally chaotic family structure, sometimes held together by rigid rules and expectations. The offender may be rather compliant, withdrawn, and isolated from peers. Asocial behavior is more likely than antisocial behavior. There may well be gender-identity or sexual-preference confusion. There may also be a generalized preference for nonsexual contact with younger children.

We are struck by a picture of low self-esteem and inadequacy in the youthful offender, particularly in dealing with peers. There is also a probability of school adjustment difficulties. Obviously, if there has been sexual victimization, most of these noted patterns could be exaggerated.

Risk factors or concerns that do not fit these patterns are:

1. history of violence, particularly if violence or coercion seems to be increasing;
2. substance abuse or general antisocial behavior;
3. denial of responsibility or minimization;
4. multiple offenses or victims; and
5. compulsive or ritualized sexual behaviors.

Treatment of the youthful offender utilizes elements of both victim and offender strategies. The major focus, from both, is clear responsibility and positive control.

The responsibility issue may be clouded because of the youthful offender's own victimization and because of the offender's age, so clarification of responsibility is vital. Although the offender's own victimization is acknowledged and discussed in as much detail as possible, victimization cannot be used as an excuse or rationalization for an offense. The offender must clearly accept the responsibility for the sexual behavior. This is also true regardless of age or maturity level despite possible difficulty in verbal ability. As *clearly as possible*, the youthful offender needs to take responsibility, including the details of the contact, antecedent behaviors, and impact on the victim.

These issues are best addressed in an atmosphere of supportive confrontation. This confrontation is accomplished in a combination of individual, family, and peer group modalities. Although this is similar to the supportive confrontation discussed in the "offender" section, there can generally be an added dose of optimism for the youthful offender.

The different modalities can reinforce each other, but some issues can best be handled in one or the other. Individual work can concentrate on affective awareness and expression, the offender's own victimization, control skills (thought stopping, fantasy control, antecedent control), and journal writing.

Family techniques deal with the cycles of abuse, appropriate modeling, and communication. The former two are particularly important in this age group and require cooperation from the whole family. There may be great resistance in exposing family secrets or changing behavioral patterns.

Group time can be used to develop interpersonal skills, affective expression (particularly anger work), and self-concept, and address peer concerns such as substance abuse.

An emphasis with this population is sex education. A special group should deal with sex information including psychophysiological response, psychosexual development, sexual preference, sexual identity, and responsibility for behavior including contraception and sexually transmitted diseases. Sex-role issues should be emphasized—identity, roles, stereotyping, expectations, and sexism.

The youthful offender clearly has unique concerns. Much more clinical experience and research is needed in order to address these concerns.

CHAPTER 3

INTERVENTION STRATEGIES—OFFENDER

Remember the metaphor of sexual abuse as the snow-covered volcano? Treating the offender is a lot like scaling that mountain:

- At first, the task seems impossible and one wonders why anyone would undertake it.
- Early discouragement is almost predictable.
- Two steps forward are frequently accompanied by slipping backwards.
- Obstacles are buried and may require a quick change of plans.
- The depth of the snow varies.
- Climbing is best done in teams, with experienced climbers.
- The atmosphere may remain bitter cold or there may be an early thaw.
- Most onlookers are rooting for the mountain.
- *And*, the whole thing may blow up at any time, with or without warning.

Of course, there is some reward at reaching the summit, or coming close to it. Most of the time, however, the counselor needs to gain satisfaction from simply making the journey. This chapter will focus on the segments of that journey, from assessment and crisis intervention to empowerment and risk reduction. The major focus will be on the regressed offender because that profile is encountered most frequently. Specific modifications will be noted for other dynamics.

The offender is probably going to be the only family member mandated for treatment. Although juvenile court may order the child(ren) into counseling, there are typically little or no consequences for failure to comply. On the other hand, the offender risks revocation of probation and incarceration for failure to attend counseling.

Most counselors utilize the concepts of voluntary treatment and confidentiality. Both of these concepts are limited in dealing with pedosexual issues. The offender should be clearly informed of these limitations at the beginning of treatment:

1. Attendance will be reported.
2. Progress and problems will be reported to the treatment team.
3. Violations of probation conditions or court orders will be reported.
4. Financial status (payment of fees) will be reported.
5. Any new allegations of abuse will be reported.
6. The protection of the child will *always* be the primary consideration.

In some cases, the client will have been advised by an attorney not to discuss details of an allegation until after sentencing or plea bargaining. This can be respected through the use of "hypothetical" or general discussions. Counselors will, of course, have to be aware of their own state laws regarding confidentiality or privileged communication. In some cases in local treatment programs agreement may be reached with law enforcement or prosecutors for special confidentiality. The counselor may also have to ensure that the client is represented by an attorney.

How can the counselor establish trust and rapport with these kinds of limitations? The counselor actually may perceive these as an obstacle more so than the client. The client is typically *in crisis* (pain, guilt, anxious about legal system) and in need of support, care, and information. Even the mandatory treatment becomes less of an issue as the clients become "hooked" into treatment. The clients typically grow to see the counselor as their advocate despite these limitations.

The counselor will also need to determine whether treatment (or assessment) will be isolated or integrated. Isolated treatment involves only the offender. In this situation, there may be no plans for reunification of the family or the offense may be extrafamilial. Integrated treatment includes other family members in the treatment plan, regardless of plans for reunification. Integrated treatment is almost always preferred because it builds a support system, increases the effectiveness of taking responsibility, and improves control. However, isolated *as well as* integrated therapy may occur at the same time. The offender will, no doubt, have individual issues to resolve other than the abusive behavior and how it affects the victim. The independent issues may not be appropriate for discussion within the context of family treatment. The need or possibility of this, of course, will be partially determined by the time element.

As quickly as possible, the counselor should determine whether treatment will be short- or long-term. This will depend on:

- *Incarceration.* Only a few weeks may be available until the offender goes to prison.
- *Voluntary treatment.* If there are no legal consequences, the offender and family may terminate treatment early.
- *Divorce.* If there is an early decision to divorce (and relocation of children is involved), the isolated treatment plan might be somewhat shorter.
- *Limited mandated treatment.* It is possible that the courts or CPS may order a prescribed number of sessions or time duration for treatment. It is typically unlikely that families will voluntarily continue after that time.

If it seems that short-term treatment is likely, the focus needs to be on responsibility, impact on the victim, and risk reduction. There should be heavy emphasis on cognitive/behavioral approaches rather than insight/historical approaches.

Assessment/Evaluation

The counselor may be involved in three types of assessment processes:

- *Formal/consultation.* This is a one-time or time-limited process with a goal of recommendations of various types. The counselor generally acts as a consultant in that there is no expectation of ongoing treatment with that counselor/client relationship. The types of recommendations will be discussed below.
- *Formal/ongoing.* The counselor may be asked to do part or all of a formal assessment of a client who will continue in ongoing treatment.

- *Informal/ongoing.* The counselor will be expected to provide ongoing assessment of a client in treatment. This may include diagnosis, prognosis, and treatment plan modification.

Goals of Assessment

Any of these types of assessment may be used with a variety of goals in mind:

- *Evidentiary.* Although there may be some ethical questions involved in this process, the counselor may be asked to help determine whether the accused committed the offense, what happened, and how often. As an alternative, the counselor may be asked if the accused fits the "profile" of an offender.
- *Risk assessment.* The counselor may be asked to determine various kinds of general and specific risk factors. These include the risk of a repeat offense; abuse or threat to children; violence or danger to society; suicide; or probation violation.
- *Rehabilitation potential.* A somewhat different question is whether the offender has a good potential to change his behavioral patterns. This includes the potential benefit from treatment or incarceration. It may include an analysis of the offender's resources, both internal (intelligence, personality, health) and external (friends, family, career).

The counselor should know who the client is in these consultation assessments and communicate that clearly to the accused/offender. The client may be the defense or prosecuting attorney, the court (judge), probation department, CPS, juvenile court, or the offender himself. Although the assessment will be objective regardless of the client, the information may be used differently.

Assessment for Treatment Planning

The goals might be different if the assessment is part of a treatment planning process rather than an isolated evaluation. The primary positive factor is the stability and trust inherent in the counseling relationship. Counseling presents a much better atmosphere for supportive confrontation than does an evaluation, particularly regarding responsibility issues. The offender can discuss details of the abuse and the antecedents to it without the pressure implicit in a formal evaluation.

The goals for treatment planning are interactive between the needs of the offender and the victim. If treatment is isolated, without the direct involvement of the victim, consideration can still be given to the actual and potential victim(s). Goals should be broad enough to address concerns beyond the abuse issues to general self-control, responsibility, and self-esteem.

These latter general issues are extremely important for the treatment planning process. There is a danger that treatment goals may be defined too narrowly, focusing only on the sexual offense and "assurance" of no repeated offense. Although these narow issues certainly need to be thoroughly resolved, treatment of the more general issues may be an even better predictor of overall adjustment, stability, and control, thereby lowering risk factors. Early in the treatment process, many offenders will claim that they have "learned their lesson" and "will not do it again." Even though they may be correct, they will feel much more confident, and be able to provide more specificity, when the more general issues are resolved.

Assessment Techniques

1. *Clinical interview.* Despite cautions that will be discussed later, the clinical interview is central to any assessment. The key factor, of course, is the judgment of an experienced interviewer. The interview should go beyond the typical mental status examination to include family, social, career, developmental, substance abuse, affective, and responsibility issues.

Family information should include family of origin, current family, and past marriages and families. Significant relationships that did not result in marriage should also be noted. Patterns in relationships should be probed, especially dependency and control issues. The relationship of the subject to each of the children should be supplemented by an understanding of each child's role in the family and family communication patterns.

The focus on social adjustment should include peer relationships (past and current), general relationships with women, isolative tendencies, and leisure activities. Social relationships with children should be probed, such as preference for child-oriented activities, leadership in child and youth groups/teams, or, at the other extreme, abusive hostility toward children.

Although specific careers may not be predictive of a sex offense, there may be a tendency for offenders to choose isolative or dependent job settings. Employment stability and relationships with employers and other employees should be noted.

A developmental history should include physical, cognitive, and intellectual development. A brief medical and educational history should focus on perceived areas of strengths, weaknesses, and, specifically, disability or potential rejection.

Patterns of substance use/abuse are a concern not only because of addictive behavior but also as evidence of chronic or crisis-oriented dependency. Denial and minimization should be expected and confronted, particularly among "just beer" drinkers.

Affective awareness is a critical area. Many offenders are particularly unaware of or unable to express feelings. This extends not only to relationship feelings—love, anger, resentment—but to more general feelings like sadness, frustration, and anxiety. An "affective history" should gather data on feelings throughout childhood, adolescence, and adulthood, particularly regarding patterns of affection, nurturance, and dependence.

Finally, responsibility issues should be clarified as much as possible. Ideally, the offender should be able to accept fully the responsibility for his actions. At the time of assessment, however, even those with positive prognoses may not be clearly aware of responsibility early in treatment or may be under legal obligation not to admit liability. In other words, whereas clear acceptance of responsibility is a positive predictor, the absence of it may not be a negative one.

2. *Sex history.* A structured sex history should be done separately from the clinical interview. The separation between the two helps in maintaining a systematic approach to the sex history. The history should clearly include all sexual behavior and arousal patterns, with a special focus on early sexual experiences with peers and adults. These childhood experiences should not be labeled as "molestations" or "abuse" by the interviewer in order to circumvent typical denial patterns. Fantasy patterns should be probed in a similar way because initial responses will probably be superficial and minimal.

3. *Psychometric evaluation.* As noted earlier there is considerable disagreement about the efficacy of psychometrics. Again, part of the problem is in the classification of offenders. MMPI (Minnesota Multiphasic Personality Inventory) profiles that may apply to rapists, for example, will generally not be valid for most pedosexual offenders. The MMPI may, however, be helpful in developing a general diagnostic picture and also may be helpful as a cross-check for credibility and openness versus guardedness. The

Multiphasic Sex Inventory (MSI) may be helpful in a similar manner, as a validation of the sex history. The Millon Clinical Multiaxial Inventory (MCMI-II) may be useful as an alternate or supplement to the MMPI. Projective measures may be helpful depending on the evaluator's experience, but may be more difficult to defend within the judicial system. An intellectual/cognitive measure (e.g., Wechsler Adult Intelligence Scale—WAIS-R) may be needed only if there is some question regarding ability to effectively gain from verbal therapy modalities.

4. *Psychophysiological measures.* Perhaps the most innovative work in the area of assessment has come in the form of psychophysiological measures—the penile plethysmograph and the polygraph. Although neither of these have yet been ruled as admissible evidence in court, they can provide helpful techniques in penetrating the barriers of denial and minimization (Abel & Becker, 1984; McGovern & Peters, 1988).

The plethysmograph provides a visual readout (graph or digital) of penile arousal through a transducer attached to the penis. Arousal is then measured while the subject is exposed to various stimuli—audio and visual tapes, slides, or films with various themes, both normal and "deviant," including children, nudity, rape, or seduction. Patterns of arousal are noted and explored with the subject, either while on or off the plethysmograph.

The polygraph ("lie detector") can be used as a supplement to the plethysmograph to detect arousal patterns in the general physiology as well as to detect "lies" and denial mechanisms.

Psychophysiological techniques provide useful information in the assessment process but may be even more useful in the treatment process. When used as an intrasubject measurement, the data can be used as a monitor particularly for behavioral treatment modalities. There may be considerably more validity to this approach. These data may also be critical in further research on normal and pathological response patterns.

Although these techniques are promising, there are important cautions and drawbacks to be recognized. Perhaps the most obivous is that a trained technician must administer the procedures. Besides the added complexity to the process, there is also the additional expense on top of a significant capital expense for the equipment (several thousand dollars depending on computerization options). There are also significant validity questions. Do we know enough about normal arousal? What patterns do "normal" subjects show? Does arousal predict behavior? If so, at what levels? What specific stimuli predict specific behavior?

Cautions Regarding Assessment

Assessment of accused or admitted offenders presents several unique problems. Primary among these is the dichotomy between subjects who talk "too much" and those who talk "too little." The latter is, perhaps, obvious. The subject may be facing a long prison sentence; loss of family, job, or financial security; and societal condemnation. Denial and minimization are frustrating but understandable and particularly painful when a child has to testify against a father. As prison sentences increase, the tendency, of course, will be toward more denial and less acceptance of responsibility. This affects all components of the system—from family to treatment to the criminal justice system to child protection agencies.

The other half of the dichotomy, talking "too much," is not anticipated by many counselors. There are many offenders, particularly within families, who eagerly confess to the pedosexual contact immediately on confrontation, and another group that will confess within a month of the report. Each of these groups may abrogate its own rights because of feelings of guilt and shame. In some cases, this is guilt that has been building or fermenting for years. Although this guilt release seems appropriate and could be therapeutic, it is also essentially irreversible and can result in later bitterness, resentment, and minimization.

Another caution is that despite the presence or absence of a "confession," there may be significant discrepancies in the reports, both being from one person to another and also from one time to another. These discrepancies may be normal and tolerated if they do not affect the overall responsibility issues. For example, specific dates, times, places, and frequency may be discrepant and acceptable if the nature of the behavior, extent, and duration are clear.

A typical confounding variable in the responsibility area is the claim of an alcohol- or other drug-induced blackout. Accused offenders will frequently claim vague or no memory of a pedosexual contact due to a "blackout." Some offenders will try to sidestep the responsibility issue by agreeing that they "might have" or "could have" done "something" or that "if *she* said I did it, then I must have." Others will totally deny memory and even use alcohol as a defense, claiming that they *could not* have offended because of lack of consciousness, absence from the home, or erectile incapability. Although the possibility of substance-induced amnesia should be acknowledged, many, if not most, of these cases do result in partial or total appropriate recall during the treatment process.

While waiting for this recall, the offender's responsibility for the substance use/abuse should be a clear focus. If the denial process continues, the offender may not be a candidate for treatment.

The final assessment caution lies in the potential for manipulation by the subject. This caution is also applicable to treatment. The subject may well act charming, pathetic, or passive-aggressive in an attempt to ally with the examiner and convince him or her of the need for leniency. The manipulative behavior may also serve as a self-assuaging process, actually helping to convince the offender that the behavior was not harmful or serious.

Diagnosis, Categorization, and Treatment Planning

Assessment of the offender goes beyond the typical issues of diagnosis and prognosis. Risk assessment and treatment planning are both essential components and add to the complexity and difficulty of the task. Treatment planning should be considered even if incarceration is anticipated. Integration of diagnosis and pedosexual taxonomy category should be helpful, essentially adding three axes to the diagnostic system.

Most pedosexual behavior is not specifically classified in the DSM-IIIR. The exception, as noted earlier, is pedophilia, classified as 302.20 on Axis I as one of the paraphilias. The criteria for the diagnosis of pedophilia are quite specific although less so than in the DSM-III. There are three components:

A. Over a period of at least six months, recurrent intense sexual urges and sexually arousing fantasies involving sexual activity with a prepubescent child or children (generally age 13 or younger).

B. The person has acted on these urges or is markedly distressed by them.

C. The person is at least 16 years old and at least 5 years older than the child or children in A. (APA, 1987, p. 285)

The changes from DSM-III are:

1. the duration criterion of 6 months;
2. "urges *and* fantasies" rather than "act *or* fantasy";
3. "distress" can be substituted for action;
4. 16 years old as the minimum age; and
5. focus on arousal instead of preference.

These changes seem to have counteracting tendencies to be more inclusive (arousal, distress, possibility of nonexclusive behavior) and exclusive (duration, age, intensity).

Any of the other Axis I diagnoses of the offender are possibilities, but the most likely would be in the affective disorders, sexual disorders, or substance abuse. The diagnosis of an affective disorder is difficult because of reality influences and stresses and the frequent overlay of personality disorders. For many offenders, however, there is considerable depression, perhaps chronic, that could be diagnosed as dysthymia (300.40) or major depression (296.3x).

Although sexual disorders seem a reasonable corollary of pedosexual contact, they may not be more prevalent in the offender than in the nonoffending population. Possible disorders include other paraphilias, sexual dysfunctions (ejaculatory and erectile), and compulsive sexual disorder. The latter may fit for the addictive-type offender. Compulsive behaviors could include masturbation, use of sexually explicit media or prostitutes, voyeurism, exhibitionism, or a combination. These behaviors may not meet the criteria for paraphilias but still contribute to a compulsive sexual disorder.

Substance abuse may be a diagnosable condition. Careful assessment is essential in this area because of the impact on both risk assessment and treatment planning. Specialized treatment may be needed. Beer is most likely to be the substance abused because of the typical "macho" dynamics.

Axis II diagnoses are more typical for many offenders. Dependent, narcissistic, passive-aggressive, and borderline personality disorders, or mixtures of these, are likely. This kind of long-term pattern of behavior sets the stage for the triggering dynamics and disinhibition. The dependent personality in combination with dysthymic disorder sets up a particularly strong tendency toward poor self-esteem, lack of appropriate feelings of power and control, lack of affection and affective awareness, and use of alcohol or sexual behavior to fill other needs. Interestingly, antisocial personality disorder is not a typical diagnosis; most offenders have little or no history of overt antisocial behavior. They exhibit, instead, rather rigid, conservative/traditional tendencies.

Pedosexual Taxonomy

The pedosexual taxonomy described earlier in chapter 1 can be a helpful framework because it focuses the dynamics of the pedosexual offender in a much narrower way than the DSM system can. Although, as noted, the five categories—regressed, pedophile, addicted/compulsive, rapist, symptomatic—are not completely discrete, I believe that they do separate out some factors that will assist in risk assessment.

Regressed. If the assessment does not indicate pedophilic patterns or other serious psychopathology, the offender probably fits the regressed category. There will probably be a reasonable psychosexual development with adult partners preceding the pedosexual contact. Dynamics include general stress, lack of control, poor self-esteem; history of physical or sexual abuse; marital/family dysfunction; and disinhibition factors, including alcohol use. There may well be a sense of "macho," a powerful veneer covering a sense of dependency and helplessness. Although this exists even before the pedosexual contact, it is worse after it, with the addition of significant guilt. That guilt, in turn, may trigger defense mechanisms, primarily projection and denial. Although the regressed offender presents a complex picture, prognosis for treatment is good if the offender accepts any responsibility for the behavior. Treatment will, however, be long-term and confrontive in order to deal completely with issues of responsibility, control, and power. If these issues are successfully addressed, the regressed offender will present a minimal risk of recidivism.

Pedophile. The criteria for DSM-IIIR diagnosis of pedophile also should be followed for the pedosexual taxonomy. Although the term "preferred" was eliminated in the shift from DSM-III to IIIR, it may still be a good operative word in exploring pedophile dynamics. Not only do pedophiles prefer children as sexual objects, they *generally* prefer to be with children and feel more comfortable with children than with adults. As one pedophile client (case study D) succinctly summarized, "I love children. I *really* love children." Although criteria call for at least a 6-month duration, most pedophiles will acknowledge almost a lifelong preference (at least a general preference) for children. They frequently will present as kind, gentle, and generous individuals who may be seen as the best babysitter or caregiver in the neighborhood, giving gifts and taking children to the circus, zoo, and so forth. Although they may have had some adult sexual relationships, including marriage, they remain essentially asexual in regard to adults. Pedophiles may be more likely than regressed offenders to choose male children. Caution should be used with the term "homosexual pedophile" because the preference is very different than that of the adult homosexual. The pedophile may find great difficulty in focusing on responsibility and frequently sees nothing wrong with his behavior and sees no harm done to the children, frequently considering his gentle concern and affection toward children as superior to the childs' parents' hostility or apathy. Because of this difficulty with responsibility as well as the long-term preference, exclusivity, and urge intensity, the pedophile is generally seen as being at high risk for recidivism. Even when the pedophile is cooperative with treatment, mandated or voluntary, treatment efficacy generally has been poor.

The special case of the hebephile/ephebophile should be noted. For the purposes of the pedosexual taxonomy, these two categories are included in the pedophile area. These categories are not specifically included in the DSM-IIIR but are generally included in the paraphilias. Both are difficult to differentiate from normal arousal patterns because of our societal emphasis on the attractiveness of youth. The hebephile sees the female adolescent as having adult development but vulnerability. There may also be a sense of safety from rejection because the hebephile may have had actual or perceived poor sexual performance with adult partners. The ephebophile is even more likely to reflect the emphasis on youth in society; in this case, the gay culture's emphasis on youthful appearance. It should be emphasized, of course, that whereas many or most adults are attracted to the youthful appearance of the male or female adolescent, the hebephile/ephebophile not only takes action on that attraction but has a preferred or exclusive arousal pattern. In other words, whereas the societal youth emphasis is a factor in attraction to adolescents, it is not *the* reason for pedosexual arousal patterns. Unfortunately, the offender may well use this as a rationalization and, like the pedophile, show little responsibility or acknowledgment of harm to the victim. Because of this, the hebephile/ephebophile also may present a significant risk.

Addicted/compulsive. The sex addict or compulsive is marked by the sense of a loss of control over sexual behavior. Any sexual behavior or combination of behaviors may be the compulsive focus. Masturbation and use of sexually-explicit media may be the most common behavior, with voyeurism, exhibitionism, and use of prostitution as other possibilities. Other nonsexual addictions are likely, including alcoholism and eating disorders. Pedosexual contact may not be one of the most frequent behaviors among these offenders, but may become more of a focus as we learn more about the addictive/compulsive patterns. As mentioned, the sex history should bring out this information, although the emphasis should not be on either specific behavior or frequency, but rather on the sense of lack of control over the behaviors. With clear acknowledgment of responsibility (not only guilt or remorse), prognosis for treatment may well be good, particularly if specialized treatment is available. Even with this prognosis, however, there may be significant risk concerns. These risks may not be related primarily to the pedosexual contact but rather to other sexual and nonsexual risk behaviors, from voyeurism to drunk driving to cocaine sales to substance-related theft.

Rapist. The key behavior pattern of the rapist is violence. The typical risk dynamics of rape are magnified when we consider children as victims. Given our current lack of treatment efficacy with rapists in general, the pedosexual rapist is an extremely high-risk offender for both sexual and physical assault.

Symptomatic. Prognosis and risk assessment for the symptomatic offender depend on the primary disorder. The frequency and type of pedosexual contact may be strong factors, however, in risk assessment. As in other areas, the ability and willingness to take responsibility are major issues.

Treatment Planning

If the consensus of the evaluation, risk assessment, and the criminal justice system indicates treatment rather than long-term incarceration, the counselor may become a critical part of the treatment planning process. This process probably will be ongoing and integrated, with the probation department and Child Protective Services both likely to have input. Although the process will be dynamic over time, it will identify modalities, intervention approaches, and goals. Timelines, frequently used in treatment planning for other types of interventions, should be flexible and individualized. Regular treatment planning meetings, preferably formal and scheduled (with room for emergencies and crises), should be held to revise the treatment plan.

Treatment of the pedosexual offender is best when it is multimodal and when more than one therapist is involved. The presence of a therapy team discourages controlling and manipulative behaviors by the offender and the family and may improve both flexibility and accountability in treatment. Modalities include:

1. *Individual therapy.* The individual therapist may be designated as the primary therapist and should be the most stable, long-term influence. If possible, this person should be willing to commit to long-term (at least a 2-year) direct and indirect involvement with the family. The individual therapist is also at the core of accountability.

2. *Family therapy.* Whenever possible, even if reunification is not a goal, marital and family therapy should be utilized. Specifics about family therapy approaches will be noted in chatper 4. Family therapy can be supportive, confrontive, preventive, and curative. Cotherapy should be used when possible. Marital therapy should also include sex education and therapy.

3. *Group therapy.* Groups are essential in the treatment process for both support and confrontation (responsibility) issues. Groups can be segregated to offenders or, at a later point, include spouses. They should be homogeneous for pedosexual offenders and probably for regressed offenders as well.

4. *Self-help.* Many offenders and families gain socialization skills, practical and emotional support, and information from self-help organizations like Parents United. This group, founded in San Jose, California, as part of Giaretto's integrated treatment program (1982), now has chapters across the country, empowering families to help themselves, elect their own officers, and regain a sense of control over their lives.

5. *Educational groups.* Particularly in the later stages of treatment, educational groups can focus on issues like communication, parenting, and sexuality.

Specific intervention approaches include:

1. *Therapeutic-behavioral, cognitive, cognitive-behavioral, rational-emotive, and eclectic.* Behavioral (desensitization) approaches may include monitoring with the plethysmograph or other psychophysiological measures.

2. *Psychopharmacological.* This approach may include standard antidepressant and tranquilizer medication if appropriate, although few offenders seem to have received this. In fact, "self-medication," particularly with alcohol, may be more likely than prescribed medication. One controversial treatment has been the use of an anti-androgen, medroxaprogesterone acetate (Depo-provera), sometimes called "chemical castration." Despite reports of success with some offenders, it is still generally considered a treatment of last resort.

3. *Probation.* Supervised probation is one of the interventions for many offenders. Although some clinicians may not see probation

as an intervention in the typical sense, it clearly has a major impact on the offender and his family, particularly as it applies to issues of power and control. Probation may be supervised at various levels of control, from monitoring by monthly report to surveillance and continued telephone accounting. Technological advances may include electronic "banding" and monitoring. The court will issue conditions of probation specifying restrictions on travel, visitation, and other behavior.

4. *Jail.* The offender may be ordered to spend some time in incarceration as a condition of, or precursor to, probation. Sentences may vary from 30 days to 2 years and may include special programs such as work furlough or weekday release to allow continued employment and family support. The imposition of "jail time" generally is intended to have a punitive, rather than therapeutic, effect, but it can be a significant intervention (positive or negative) regarding power and control issues.

Treatment goals will vary, but certain goals seem consistent despite modalities and specific interventions. I have grouped these into six areas: responsibility, power, control, affective awareness, communication, and interpersonal relationships.

Responsibility. The offender will:

- clearly accept the responsibility for the pedosexual contact without reservation or rationalization;
- clearly acknowledge the actual and potential harm to the victim, himself, and the family;
- accept the ongoing responsibility for support and protection of the family regardless of reunification decisions;
- demonstrate responsibility in employment, finances, and similar areas;
- demonstrate responsibility in attendance and utilization of therapy opportunities;
- accept and adhere to conditions of probation and other directives of the criminal justice and child protective systems; and
- differentiate between responsibility and guilt.

Power. The offender will:

- acknowledge the inappropriate power relationship inherent in the pedosexual contact;
- identify and correct inappropriate power relationships in the family;

- identify areas of individual powerlessness and plans for change;
- assist in empowering the victim; and
- demonstrate ability to share power in the marital, familial, or work situation.

Control. The offender will:

- demonstrate control over sexual arousal, behavior, and fantasy;
- acknowledge disinhibitors and plans for controlling them;
- describe the "set-up" for the pedosexual contact and plans for controlling these (relapse prevention);
- demonstrate general impulse control, including control over "temper" and substance abuse;
- demonstrate control over day-to-day decision making for himself; and
- understand and resolve issues regarding need for control over others and relinquish this need.

Affective awareness. The offender will:

- identify the full range of his feelings consistently and with understanding;
- express the range of feelings and clarify same to the counselor and the family;
- demonstrate ability to understand, clarify, and take appropriate action on others' feelings; and
- specifically, demonstrate ability to appropriately express anger.

Communication. The offender will:

- demonstrate ability to use "I" messages and active listening;
- demonstrate ability to express and receive thoughts, feelings, opinions, and beliefs;
- develop effective extrafamilial communication (work, social, etc.); and
- demonstrate improved parenting skills.

Interpersonal relationships. The offender will:

- demonstrate improved relationship with spouse or significant other;
- demonstrate awareness of intimacy needs within relationships;

- show appropriate sexual relationship(s) with adult partner(s); and
- demonstrate improved socialization skills and reduced isolation.

Treatment

The assumptions in this discussion of treatment interventions are that most offenders will be *mandated* and available for *long-term* treatment. If either of those assumptions is not true, the treatment goals will have to be modified, with an emphasis on crisis intervention, responsibility, and control. As in the treatment of victims, the stages of treatment for offenders are overlapping and flexible. Crises, for example, *will* occur throughout the process up to, and beyond, formal termination. The stages will be roughly parallel in either an individual or group modality.

Crisis Intervention

As noted earlier, all of the major family members (victim, offender, spouse) should be considered suicide risks. Even while denying allegations in the initial stages, the offender may attempt to resolve conflicting feelings by suicide. Clearly, any attempt could be devastating for the victim and family.

At the time of the report and arrest, more so than at later times, the offender is likely to perceive issues as "black and white." The counselor can use this black-and-white perspective with a clear treatment contract, including a suicide contract. Because many offenders have dependent features, the most effective suicide prevention may be in telling the offender, "Don't do it!"

For the most part, however, the counselor needs to emphasize and validate the gray area—that there will be few easy and clear answers. The initial crisis phase will be marked by extreme confusion and fear. Information received by the family will usually be ambiguous and elicit many questions—will the child be removed, the father arrested or prosecuted, siblings removed, the father incarcerated? The counselor will not be able to answer these questions and obviously should not make any promises about outcomes. In fact, the counselor should acknowledge and even emphasize that the family does *not* have control over these decisions but, rather, they have to focus their efforts on the small amount of control that they *do* have. This is a critical reframing.

As noted earlier, the offender is likely to enter this phase in a denial mode either by outright denial of the pedosexual contact or by minimization of the extent, frequency, duration, or effect of the contact. Even those who readily admit to the contact will have accounts that differ from the child's report, for many reasons. The offender can be supported in his need to protect himself while confronted about his need to accept responsibility for the good of his family and himself.

This concept of supportive confrontation is critical not only in this crisis phase but throughout treatment. The counselor must be able to support his or her client while still being able to confront the client on issues of responsibility, control, and accountability. The counselor consistently must walk the thin line of concern for the client and responsibility to the victim. One technique for accomplishing this is to ally with the offender in his concern for the victim. Most offenders are cooperative in this regard, making it somewhat easier to deal with responsibility issues.

As part of the support, the offender can be assured that he is not the only one in this circumstance. Despite the heavy, negative societal condemnation and, more than likely, tremendous self-condemnation, the offender can be shown that his and his family's problems are not unique and that many families have recovered. Without diluting any responsibility for the offense, the counselor can show unconditional positive regard and reinforce the basic "OK-ness" of the offender. In most cases, the offender's lack of previous criminal record can be helpful, as can an emphasis on the previously mentioned alliance to protect the victim.

Once that support is given, responsibility becomes the biggest issue of the crisis phase. The offender *must* clearly accept responsibility for the offense. This is probably the most important treatment goal in the whole process. The responsibility must be unequivocal; that is, without excuses or rationalizations. The responsibility must go beyond a simple acknowledgment of the behavior. It must include the set-up, statements of threat, coercion, and confusion made to the victim, damage to himself and others, and consequences (jail, probation, separation of the offender's family). There can, and probably will be, specific differences in details between the "stories" of the offender and the victim. These differences can be explored during treatment *if* the basic responsibility is clearly accepted. The offender may need several sessions and considerable supportive confrontation in order to accomplish this.

The responsibility issue should be addressed in a positive manner, the emphasis being that responsibility allows the treatment process to begin. Responsibility, in a positive way, becomes the best route for the offender to take control of the treatment process and establish the first step in a more general positive control. The positive responsibility emphasis is in contrast to the disabling guilt that many, if not most, offenders feel. Although a certain amount of guilt is to be expected, it becomes self-destructive and counterproductive unless the counselor can turn it around into positive responsibility.

Apology Sessions

The apology sessions become the bridge from crisis intervention to ongoing treatment. The number of sessions and timing will be flexible. The goals will be responsibility clarification, apology, validation of the report, and commitment to treatment.

As noted earlier, the apology sessions will not take place until both victim and offender are prepared, with emphasis on the victim's safety and support. Preparation for the offender should focus on the responsibility issues and enough affective awareness to clearly respond to the victim's feelings. Role-playing is one method to prepare the offender for a variety of victim responses, from coldness to rage.

The offender will be expected to initiate the first apology session by acknowledging the complete responsibility for the offense and apologizing for the contact. The victim will then be encouraged to respond with feelings or questions. The offender *will* accept *any* feelings expressed by the victim. These feelings, of course, may be expressed over the course of several sessions. The other goals should be accomplished in the first session (although they may be repeated): The report should be validated as appropriate and the first step in "making things better," and the offender should make a firm commitment to treatment and to making whatever changes are necessary for the victimized family to recover and for the victim to be safe.

Continuing apology sessions should focus on including the rest of the offender's family, especially the spouse. Apologies should be directed to other family members, with clear acknowledgment of the harm inflicted. The details of the contact should be discussed in order to have an improved sense of protection and in order to disrupt the "family secret" pattern.

If the offender's family is not available for apology sessions, the process should still be completed using role-play (perhaps with another counselor) or letter writing. If only the children are not available, the apology sessions should be held with the spouse with, again, the details of the contact discussed, even if the spouse is not initially eager to hear them.

Pattern Analysis

Once responsibility issues have been clarified and communicated, the major treatment tasks involve pattern analysis. This includes an understanding of individual and systems dynamics, history, disinhibition, arousal patterns, and affective awareness.

As much as possible, the offender should bear the responsibility for work on pattern analysis. The counselor should facilitate the process and be accountable for progress toward the treatment goals, as well as for integration of the patterns.

The pattern analysis may be the biggest part of the jigsaw puzzle analogy mentioned earlier. The offender must painstakingly put together the puzzle, sometimes piece by piece, somtimes several pieces in a cluster. The counselor can understand how puzzles fit together but doesn't know how this particular one will look. And, the puzzle may never have all the pieces in place.

The first step in putting together the puzzle is to clearly identify the pieces. The offender must be able to discuss the details of the pedosexual contact and identify the direct antecedents to the contact. This is sometimes called the "set-up" or "seduction," although the latter is not an accurate description when viewed in the typical adult way. The details should include frequency and duration as well as progressive patterns (stroking to digital penetration to oral-genital contact). Victim and offender responses should be queried. Offender techniques for convincing the child not to tell should be elicited. Offender arousal patterns during the contact should be as specific as possible (how much of an erection, at what point, for how long?). Information regarding time and place will help to determine how protection mechanisms (e.g., rest of family) were circumvented. Finally, the offender should clearly understand how the report came about.

After the details of the contact have been determined, disinhibiting factors should be considered. These factors include any that clearly serve to disinhibit the offender from sexual contact with children. Disinhibiting factors may be relatively overt, like alcohol use/misuse; or more subtle, like elaborate rationalizations. The latter may include the child's "need for sex education," "need for affection," or "medical necessity." They also may include a child's initiating, enjoying, or demanding contact, spousal rejection, or the child's being asleep. One of the great ironies is that the offender could use the contact as punishment for sexual behavior such as normal childhood masturbation or peer exploration. Multiple disinhibition factors are likely to be present.

The disclosure of details and disinhibiting factors may take a considerable amount of time. Just like the process of sorting out and turning over pieces of a puzzle, it may seem like a nonproductive and time-consuming effort, but it does unravel patterns and helps to "hook" the puzzle solver into the task.

One strategy for completing a puzzle is to identify the straight-edged pieces and complete the outer perimeter. This accomplishes three purposes: It establishes the outer limits and dimensions, sets a structure for at least some of the patterns, and provides positive reinforcement and encouragement by narrowing the number of possible combinations and by making connections. In the pattern analysis, this phase examines the individual's family and sexual history.

The offender will be encouraged to look at his family(ies) of origin with an emphasis on patterns of power, dependence, control, communication, discipline, and affection. The parental marital dyad will be discussed with an emphasis on models of affection, intimacy, and sexuality. Many offenders will describe a rather rigid, nonaffectionate family with either an absent or authoritarian father, physical abuse or, at least, a strong punishment orientation. In my informal clinical research, fewer than 10% of offenders have reported *any* physical affection from their fathers (hugs, strokes, shoulder pats, lap sitting). An autobiography may be a helpful technique in gathering this information.

The sex history should be structured so that the counselor can feel assured that it is as complete as possible. It seems obvious that the possibility of a history of sexual abuse should be thoroughly pursued. Many interviewers, however, end their pursuit by asking the question, "Were you ever molested or sexually abused?" Most offenders will answer this question negatively because they do not think of their early experiences as abusive. The more helpful prompt might be, "Tell me about early sexual experiences you had with an adult or a much older child." This can be followed by a discussion of details and reactions, both past and current. The offender can be encouraged to reframe such experiences as abuse if the counselor considers it might be helpful. The sex history should also look at behavioral and fantasy arousal patterns, including masturbation and use of sexually explicit media.

The sex history and arousal patterns in most regressed offenders will tend to seem quite normal but limited. Homophobia is typical, as is a small number of close heterosexual relationships. Sexually explicit media may be a disinhibiting factor, but not to the extent that they are a factor for the pedophile or rapist and generally not with children as objects. Concerns to be explored fully include fantasy patterns involving children, adolescents, or particularly young or small women; also, fantasy patterns of control over partners, including instruction and experimentation. Force, if present, magnifies these concerns.

If arousal patterns, either during childhood or during the pedosexual contact, are of concern, the counselor might consider two options: psychophysiological assessment/treatment and fantasy control. In the former, the use of the plethysmograph can both assess and monitor treatment as a feedback measure. With or without the plethysmograph, arousal and fantasy patterns can be controlled through aversive conditioning (use of noxious stimuli such as smelling salts or use of visualizations), masturbatory satiation, or thought-stopping. Typically, these techniques would be utilized by specially trained therapists.

Once the background issues have defined the perimeter of the puzzle, the next strategy may be to group the puzzle pieces by color and shades of color to see if designs can be perceived. It should be noted, of course, that the puzzle process is not rigidly sequenced, so that some pattern/color grouping may occur while the perimeter is being assembled.

The colors are supplied by the awareness and clarification of individual and systems dynamics. Individual dynamics include personality and affective awareness and exploration of functional and dysfunctional behaviors. Typical dynamics include dependent and passive-aggressive personality patterns. These need to be continually challenged by the counselor, not in terms of right versus wrong or black versus white but in terms of productivity and effectiveness. Although all these dynamics may not need to be changed, the offender will have to become aware of their role in helping to set up or disinhibit the sexual behavior. Most offenders do change their behavior significantly, although they still may meet criteria for personality disorders. The *awareness* of these dynamics may be more important than major behavioral changes.

Along with recognizing behavioral patterns, the offender must be able to demonstrate affective awareness. It would not be unusual for an offender, when asked to describe a feeling, to respond, "I feel like it's all your fault." Integration of sensory and affective awareness may be a totally new concept as will the separation of thoughts and feelings. Many offenders report crying for the first time since childhood or for the first time *ever*. Permission to cry can be an effective lead-in to permission for feeling appropriately angry, sad, hurt, and so forth.

Dynamics may be important in any one of several systems that affect and are affected by the offender. The family system is obviously central, but employment, social, and extended family systems also may be important. The offender should become aware of roles, interactions, expectations, and other typical systems dynamics. Family systems issues will be discussed specifically in chapter 4. One critical relationship issue should be stressed, however. The offender seems to have particular difficulty in handling intimacy, both within the marital or sexual relationship as well as in friendship and extended family systems. Concepts of vulnerability, trust, and openness may be difficult and require considerable counselor patience.

One last pattern to explore specifically is substance use/abuse. Not only should this pattern be looked at in terms of disinhibition but also in terms of personality, relationship, and life-style issues. Although most offenders may not have addictive patterns, at least not yet, substance use, particularly beer consumption, has a significant impact on isolative and insulative behaviors, passivity, rationalizations, and, of course, finances.

Throughout all this pattern analysis, as in the previous phases, there has to be a recurring emphasis on responsibility, power, and control. These three underlying factors may be the most important in initially having created the problem through their inappropriate use, in acting as change agents, and in ensuring the prevention of relapse.

Empowerment

Responsibility and control issues have been discussed with some emphasis. The third major factor, power, is frequently misunderstood because the abuse of power may, correctly, be one of the key factors in facilitating the pedosexual contact.

The inequity of power within the family is exemplified by the great irony of intrafamilial sexual abuse—the offender feels powerless for a combination of reasons at the same time as he perceives the child as powerful and tries to "fight fire with fire" by using sexual contact as a power tool—so, the powerless offender becomes powerful and then, after the report, again powerless. One of the major treatment tasks is to empower the offender in order to produce an equitable power balance within the family and improve related issues such as self-esteem, independence, and self-confidence.

Empowerment goes hand-in-hand with control issues. Independence and assertiveness can be encouraged through decision-making skills, option exploration, and negotiation skills. Within the family, particular attention can be paid to parenting and financial issues, both of which are closely identified with power. Outside the family, empowerment can take the form of outreach to others, either generally or specifically within the pedosexual self-help programs.

Career issues also can be the focus of empowerment. Many offenders have had a history of unemployment, underemployment, and serial employment resulting in both economic and psychological problems. Many also will lose their jobs as a result of arrest, conviction, or incarceration. Career exploration, decision making, and stability therefore become empowerment possibilities.

Termination

Even a seemingly clear-cut issue like termination is complex. There may be several different points that seem like terminations: family reunification, CPS case closure, "graduation" from self-help programs, release from mandated treatment, or release from probation. For our purposes, we will focus on termination from treatment, although the other points also deserve much positive attention.

Because most offender treatment is mandated, termination decisions involve more than the completion of treatment goals. The treatment team will have to agree, sometimes unanimously, on the demonstration of those treatment goals and, of course, be convinced the risk of repeated offense is minimal. The termination process may include an independent reevaluation, clinical or psychophysiological.

It should be emphasized that in assessing risk of repeated offense, the risk can never be considered nonexistent. Even in the best situations, the risk will be seen as "minimal." Essentially, the treatment team must determine not only an offender's consistent compliance with the treatment goals but also an ongoing commitment to change and self-monitoring. The offender should also be able to show an ongoing support system.

The offender's commitment should include a clear agreement to return to treatment after termination as necessary. The most successful cases in my experience have returned at least once after termination to deal with a new problem. In contrast, about half of the incidents of repeated offense occur after termination and all have been related to a resumption of substance abuse behaviors. If the offender remains on probation after termination, the probation department should conduct regular urinalysis and possible psychophysiological measures.

Other Pedosexual Forms

In describing treatment strategies, we have intentionally focused on the regressed offender because that is the type of offender most counselors and therapists encounter most frequently. Many of the same interventions are appropriate for other pedosexual offenders, but some specific issues should be emphasized.

Pedophile. Responsibility and control issues are critical with the pedophile and need to be emphasized in every session. If at all possible, arousal patterns should be consistently monitored. If treatment is to be successful with the pedophile, those patterns will have to be shifted completely. The pedophile will also have to alter his pattern of nonsexual contact with children, in most cases an extremely difficult task. Research in the treatment of pedophiles will have to continue from correctional facilities, with all of the attendant difficulties that entails.

Rapist. The dynamics of the rape situation and its issues of violence generally call for specialized training, based on the experience of clinicians in the corrections field (Groth, 1979). Although the dynamics of rape are becoming better understood, most offenders have difficulty acknowledging responsibility. Child rapists may be even more difficult to treat, although research does not indicate that clearly.

Addictive/compulsive. Treatment of the addictive offender is still in the early stages, but it seems that a "12-step recovery program" may be helpful and effective. Inpatient programs, similar to other addiction programs, also have been established. For the pedosexual offender, coordinated treatment between an addictions specialist and the primary counselor seems necessary. As with the regressed offender, group treatment is helpful, if not necessary.

Symptomatic. The key element in treating the symptomatic offender is coordination between treatment team members dealing with the primary disorder and those dealing with the sexual contact. Clearly, the relationship between the primary disorder and the symptomatic pedosexual contact should be thoroughly understood.

Female offender. If there is one area that needs extensive research most, it is the phenomenon of the female offender. Although our data, as previously noted, continue to point to an overwhelming percentage of male offenders (with both male and female victims), clinical experience with adult offenders/survivors leads to the conclusion that many unreported contacts involve female offenders. Offenses by female offenders may still not approach the frequency of those by male offenders but may be more frequent than currently reported.

The major statistical factor, of course, is that male victims do not report as often as female victims because they are less likely to perceive pedosexual contact as abusive, and female children report abuse by adult women even less frequently. Many offenders report sexual contact as children from babysitters or aunts, but relatively few situations directly involving a natural mother. These situations seem to entail a major problem with substance abuse, leading to the conclusion that the offender was in a symptomatic pattern or that unusually strong disinhibition was necessary.

As an interesting sidenote, based on limited numbers, it has been our observation that female offenders are less frequently charged, convicted, or incarcerated. It is certainly not clear whether this is a pattern of reverse bias in the criminal justice system or a quirk.

Treatment of the female offender can be similar to that of the male offender. Typical issues of nurturance, intimacy, and dependency should be explored fully as should possible victimization history. Disinhibiting factors require extra attention. The basic goals of responsibility, power, and control are essentially identical to those for the male offender, although the female perspective in our society should obviously be taken into consideration.

Warnings and Cautions During Treatment

As noted in the assessment phase, the offender has many good reasons for denial and minimization of the offense as he faces sentencing. This continues to be a risk during treatment although less so after sentencing. What *does* continue is a tendency to *generally* minimize problems and emphasize progress in counseling. Vague comments such as "I'm feeling better" or "Our communication has improved" or "I won't do it again" should be challenged and confronted with a statement like "Tell me *exactly* how." Most offenders and their families (including the victim) are "ready" to terminate counseling after a few months, but when looking back with hindsight at the actual termination time, they see how much additional progress they have made.

A related issue is that an offender with a dependent personality will eagerly cooperate and say exactly what the counselor wants to hear. The offender's question, in fact, is specific: "What do you want me to tell you?" This, of course, fits right into the black-and-white, rigid pattern of the offender's pathology.

The length of treatment itself frequently becomes a therapeutic issue. The counselor will be under significant pressure to reduce the length. This pressure may come from the victim, offender, or nonoffending spouse. There also may be financial pressures on either the private practice or agency counselor to limit treatment duration. The best metaphor I've used to deal with this issue is that whereas 90% is wonderful as a "grade," this situation requires 99%, and that takes time, even beyond what seems like compliance with the treatment goals.

CHAPTER 4

INTERVENTION STRATEGIES—THE FAMILY AND ADULT SURVIVORS

Intervention Strategies—The Family

As we have discussed, most pedosexual contact occurs within the family in what has become known as intrafamilial child sexual abuse. This chapter discusses ways in which the whole family can recover from the devastation of sexual abuse and provides the most effective strategy for breaking the cycle of abuse.

The focus on the family does not necessarily imply that dysfunctional families cause abuse nor does it ignore a child's being victimized outside the family or the possibility that the offender also may seek a pedosexual contact outside the family. It also in no way removes responsibility from the offender for his behavior or excuses it. Simply, a family systems approach can be an effective treatment intervention because it also functions as a preventive approach, preventing another contact within and outside the family, preventing the intergenerational cycle from repeating, and preventing at least some other problems aside from sexual ones through improved family functioning.

The family systems strategy is effectively conceptualized by Friedman (1988), who reviewed that and other models of family intervention. Some of those concepts are integrated in this dis-

111

cussion. Before we look specifically at systems concepts, however, it will be helpful to highlight two specific roles that have not yet been discussed: the mother/spouse role and the sibling role.

The Other Victims

Although, for convenience, we refer to *the* victim as the one who has been involved in the pedosexual behavior with an adult, it would not be incorrect to view the other family members similarly, if not equally, as victims. Although this may include extended family members, friends, and associates, we will focus on the mother/spouse and sibling roles.

The offender and victim both have major issues to resolve and heal, but the mother probably has numerically *more* significant issues than either. These are emotional and logistical (and the impact of the latter should not be discounted).

The major dilemma for the mother, of course, is the schism of loyalty to her husband and protection of her child. An image is conjured of being glued to both sides of a vise—there is fear of being pulled apart and, at the same time, fear of being crushed by the force. The dilemma will last at some level, through and beyond the treatment process, from "Whom do I believe?" to "Can I ever leave them alone?"

The mother's initial dilemma arises in dealing with the report. Disbelief is probably her most common reaction. Even if there were previous suspicions, it is still difficult to believe that the sexual behavior happened. Mother will undoubtedly question the child about details in order to test credibility. There will typically be differences in the details given by offender and victim. Most mothers will believe the victim but with a great variance in how long that takes—from a few hours to several months. The question of "belief," however, is not as important as the sense of protection. The mother may have doubts and confusion about what happened but can still act to protect the child by having the father move out, cooperating with CPS, supporting the victim, and so forth.

Even after enough details are known to "convince" the mother, the feeling of being torn will continue. The mother can be encouraged to provide support for both husband and child *and* express the appropriate feelings such as anger, rage, and hurt. Whenever possible, the mother can give priority protection to the child *and* not be forced into choosing between the two loved ones. In some situations, of course, the mother may choose between victim and offender, and the treatment plan can be modified to adapt to that.

It is easy to lose track of one important consideration amid this chaos of feeling torn. The mother frequently feels guilty or responsible for the pedosexual contact. She feels that she must not have been a "good enough" sexual partner or a good wife and mother generally. She reasons that had she done better, her husband would have been satisfied or the child would have come to her for help. This feeling may be reinforced if the details refer to sexual behavior that the wife refused to do (e.g., oral sex) or if contact with the child occurred right after she declined sex or when she was ill or disabled. The issue of offender responsibility must be *strongly* emphasized.

The mother may well go through cycles of intense anger and depression. She will not only be angry at her husband but will also be angry at the child and, most of all, at herself for not protecting her child and not "seeing it coming." Her depression will primarily result from her sense of hopelessness, helplessness, and lack of control. Individual and group therapy should focus not only on these issues but also on the opportunity for her to explore issues related to her family of origin, including the possibility of having been herself a victim of either sexual or physical abuse.

Finally, the issues of logistical pressures on the mother should not be overlooked. Essentially, in most situations, she becomes an instant single mother. With a good chance of father or children being out of the home, reduced income, increased expenses, and transportation to several therapy sessions a week, the logistical and economic strains alone are formidable. Mothers will need as much support as possible with these issues.

Siblings who actually have no knowledge of the abuse start out in a position that seems to be in contrast to the mother's. Rather than feeling central to all the emotional and logistical struggles, siblings frequently feel "out of it." They may feel like they are the last to know, having caught only part of the information being discussed. Neither the victim nor the parents are eager to reveal the details to them. They are typically ignored in treatment strategies, child protective services, and the judicial system during the crisis phase except for being questioned about whether they were abused or whether they were witnesses. Even after this questioning, they frequently still don't know what is really happening.

When the details are brought out, the siblings will invariably not believe the victim. Like the mother, they feel a loyalty to the father, but even more than in her case, there is clear dependence on him and fear of abandonment if or when he is removed from the home or incarcerated. They will then, even after believing, go through a stage of "blaming the victim," reasoning that things would still be "normal" if the report had not been made. The apology sessions, which should include the siblings, must clearly address these issues.

At times, siblings *do* know or strongly suspect that abuse is occurring but may protect themselves or others by denial. They then may feel disloyal to the identified victim and may experience guilt, which is exhibited by withdrawal, anger, or confusion. Supportive therapy is necessary to help these siblings to reveal their knowledge or suspicions and rebuild the sibling relationship. They should also be helped to realize that they were victims in their own right.

It is only after these stages that the siblings may show the fear or concern that they are, or could have been, victims themselves. Their protection system—mother, counselor, CPS, probation, teacher—should specifically be identified to them and an age-appropriate agreement to go to these people must be obtained.

Family Treatment Goals

Family treatment goals can be established to parallel those of the offender and victim. These can be established somewhat independently of reunification decisions and be flexible enough to change if the reunification option changes. If the decision is made to stay separate, the family still will need considerable counseling/ support. Ideally, the father can still be a part of the family sessions. Unfortunately, in too many cases, the mother opts for a divorce and, perhaps, relocation with no therapeutic follow-up.

Family treatment goals should, minimally, include:

1. clear understanding of the details of the pedosexual contact;
2. clear acknowledgment of offender responsibility and cessation of blaming the victim;
3. improved communication, including affective communication, and clear role boundaries;
4. appropriate power relationships with a focus on mutual cooperation, and firm, but not dictatorial, parental control;
5. Appropriate sharing of responsibility for day-to-day functioning;
6. ability to have fun together; and
7. reduction of family isolation by socialization with other families or organizations.

Family Characteristics

To expand upon family dynamics discussed previously, the sexually abusive family may have the following tendencies:

1. An overly dependent yet unclear marital relationship may prevail. Each partner may be unable to meet his or her own needs and, yet, unsuccessfully tries to please the other, at least early in the relationship. The sexual relationship may suffer because of intimacy problems but, in and of itself, may be no worse than that of most couples. Clearly, offenders do not seek out children because of isolated sexual problems in their relationship.

2. The child takes on a pseudoadult role in an effort to make peace in the family. Intentionally or not, the child gains significant inappropriate power that leads to anxiety and, in turn, an increased drive for power.

3. Lack of appropriate role boundaries can be created because of one or more of the dynamics noted earlier—dictatorial father, irresponsible/dependent father, or pseudoadult child.

4. The family becomes enmeshed and therefore isolated from other social contacts. This is related to perceived risks of rejection, failure, or abandonment.

Interventions

Although some therapists emphasize the need for family treatment as the first and primary modality, it has been my experience that initiating family treatment too early may add to the confusion and dilute responsibility, making it less effective than at a later point. With the exception of the apology sessions, the focus for the first year or more of treatment should be on the individuals involved—offender, victim, mother, siblings—with a progression toward family therapy through the use of dyad/triad or subsystem therapy. Returning to the jigsaw puzzle metaphor, even though the goal is to form the big picture, it has to happen by putting two pieces together, over and over.

Dyads. There are three critical dyads in the family system—mother-child, husband-wife, and father-child. Dyad sessions with these three combinations, in that order, should begin as soon as the crisis phase is under control and after preparation of the child. Sessions may take place with one or two therapists.

Mother-child. This dyad is addressed first because of the need for clear lines of protection. The child should feel that the mother believes enough to provide that kind of safety. There is a deeper, longer-term goal of bonding or rebonding this relationship. Frequently, there has been a sense of competition and, even, jealousy rather than bonding. Trust, vulnerability, and issues of fear of abandonment or rejection need to be emphasized. A clear understanding must be established that the child will report sexual, or other, problems to the mother and that the mother will listen and take appropriate action regardless of the consequences.

Marital dyad. Clearly, the marital dyad will be a major focus of treatment. Ideally, this will be true even if there is a decision against reunification. Initially, the focus should be on both information and feelings regarding the report. The wife should be encouraged to express her rage, hurt, and fears, and the husband encouraged to accept and validate those feelings without excuses as part of his acceptance or responsibility. Each can be encouraged to "take care of self" in expressing feelings, needs, and concerns, including ways of asking for help and support without dependence. There will be a recurring emphasis on communication techniques, particularly active listening and "I messages." Mutual analysis of each other's history and dynamics will be revealing and helpful (what did I learn in my individual sessions?). Parenting issues, especially information on normal development and new options for child-rearing, are essential. Discussions should also focus on more gender-equitable sharing of responsibility, power, and control within the dyad and within the family.

Sex therapy is an absolutely essential component of the dyad work even if the couple reports no initial complaints about their sexual functioning. If possible, there should also be a sexuality class/group as part of the treatment program. Not unlike in most nonabusive situations, the couple probably has little or no information about their sexuality. Counseling and educational components should include information on anatomy and physiology, human sexual responses, psychosexual development, alternative life styles, values/beliefs, sexual dysfunction, and communication. Typically, these couples demonstrate a narrow range of behaviors, lack of sexual communication, reluctance to experiment/explore, and lack of sensuality and intimacy. If sexual dysfunction is present, it is probable that it would be ejaculatory timing, absence of orgasm or, perhaps, lack of desire.

Father-child. The most delicate dyad to deal with may also be the most rewarding. As noted in chapter 2, this relationship needs to be totally redefined. The father must regain a clear parental role, with appropriate power, in making decisions and setting limits for all the children but, particularly, for the victim. It should be specified that the victim cannot use the threat of a report to avoid reasonable paternal discipline. Appropriate affection should not only be discussed but specifically demonstrated, with feedback from the child as to comfort level of certain behaviors (e.g., hugs, kisses, sitting close, shoulder hugs). Father should specifically encourage and validate the child's creation of protection and support systems and clarify changes he has made.

Triads. The triad of child, mother, and father should meet with some regularity during the second half of the treatment process to act as a check and monitor unit. The triad may be similar to an executive committee in an organization. The individuals can accomplish a great deal as a small group but they also function as monitors to make sure progress is being made, identify problem areas and possible solutions, and confront each other in a supportive atmosphere. The triad is the ideal unit for clarifying communication and goals both among the triad and between the family and the therapists/treatment team.

The family unit. Working with the whole family unit is a significant challenge for the counselor(s), therefore the dyad/triad sessions should be a helpful preparation. The whole family should be present, although children younger than 3 or 4 could be present for only one or two sessions. Two counselors should be at each session, one of whom should clearly be the victim's advocate. Most, if not all, of the sessions should be planned for 1½ hours.

It will be helpful to initiate sessions with the children to ensure their participation. Emphasis should be placed on the rights of each person to speak and, particularly, to express feelings. This creates a model and permission for mutual respect, equity, and communication. The counselors' role is to model and guide the family in its process with a minimum of intervention, which should consist more of reinforcement and encouragement than analysis. This can be accomplished while still providing accountability for the treatment goals.

Topics for family sessions should include responsibility issues, role boundaries, self-control, support systems, household functioning (jobs, chores, projects, finances), sexual/dating concerns, work/career issues, and plans for (or results of) reunification and visits.

Visitation

One of the most effective ways of monitoring family functioning and adjustment is through the use of controlled family visitation. In this approach, the father is gradually reintroduced into the family through a long series of planned visitation sessions that are continually monitored. The goal of this controlled approach is to empower the family, particularly the mother, toward independence and self-protection.

The exact structure of the visitation process may take different forms (Wolf, Conte, & Engel-Meinig, 1988) but essentially consists of four stages: preparation, public visits, home visits, and overnight visits. Because court or probation orders may prohibit the offender to have contact with the children, the probation department has to be involved in the visitation decisions. The probation officer's presence may be a helpful controlling force.

Preparation for visits should include a set of predetermined rules for contact. The children should have a clear voice in making these rules based on their comfort level. Rules may include limitations on physical contact, agreement not to discuss the pedosexual contact, avoid arguments, and having the mother set limits and control time. One critical rule for the whole visitation process is that mother must be present and act as supervisor *at all times.* (We actually have had success with father having limited unsupervised time with the nonvictimized children late in the process.) Mother must be clearly committed to this component.

The first visits will be public (park, mall, restaurant) and last about 2 hours. Emphasis is on a positive experience; expressions of discomfort will be aired in the therapy sessions after the visits. The duration of visits will then be increased to accommodate the *most uncomfortable* member of the family. Mother's ability to control the visit will be carefully monitored.

Home visits will last, at first, about 4 hours once a week. Activities should be planned in advance with an emphasis on doing at least one "fun" thing. This time period can be increased and dinner visits added—2 hours each, once or twice a week. Home visits will gradually be increased to 8 hours on Saturdays and Sundays and 4 hours each on two to three weekdays.

Overnight visits frequently create concern among the children because mother's protection will not totally be available. Added preparation will be helpful with discussion on "how to feel safe." Options might include closed (or locked) doors, night lights, or rules against father going into children's rooms. One overnight visit, typically on the weekend, will then be checked out thoroughly before continued visits will be allowed. Overnights will then be gradually increased to four or five a week prior to considering reunification.

Reunification

For most families in the treatment program, the word "reunification" attains a new, almost mystical level of importance. It is a more important goal than terminating therapy or completing probation.

The decision for reunification is made by the treatment team when the family has completed most or all of its goals and clear safety and protection has been demonstrated in the visitation process. An indpendent reevaluation of the offender may be required. Areas for continued family improvement will be identified. All the children will be carefully questioned individually about their readiness. The family will agree to a continued treatment plan of at least 3- to 6-months' duration.

Like the other treatment interventions, family treatment is a careful, time-consuming process. Time is an important ally, allowing some problems to emerge and be resolved. Patience, again, is a most important therapeutic tool.

Interventions—Adult Survivors

We've seen many confusing dichotomies in our discussion so far—the love and hate of the victim for the father/offender, the offender's machismo and powerlessness, and the mother's conflicting loyalties. The dichotomies of the adult survivor are even more dramatic—courage and vulnerability, strength and weakness, the pain of reality and the escape of dissociation.

How do we know what we know about sexual abuse? How did we really start to understand about its extent and "the numbers"? How do we know about the damage it causes? We know because of the stories of countless courageous survivors of abuse, mostly women, who have told us not only about the behaviors but also about their fears, nightmares, compulsions, rage, and self-destructiveness.

Treatment of the adult survivor has appropriately received increasing attention in recent years. This attention has come from four somewhat disparate types of groups with similar goals: sexual abuse treatment programs, substance abuse treatment programs, rape/sexual assault recovery groups, and feminist advocacy and support groups. Although approaches may differ, the similar goals include confronting the issue, clarification of responsibility, stabilization, and positive control.

A special note should be made regarding the feminist perspective. Both female and male counselors should not only be aware of this perspective but utilize the many positive factors involved. Although most counselors of adult survivors have typically and understandably been women, the sensitive male counselor can provide a helpful model and balance to treatment. Treatment teams might be an effective tool as well. There is also, I believe, a great benefit to be gained if the counselor of adult survivors also has experience with child victims and offenders.

As noted earlier, I have intentionally separated the terms "victim" and "survivor." I believe the term "victim" can be a helpful way to emphasize the child's powerlessness, whereas "survivor" puts a positive focus on the person who has been living with this issue, whether the person has or has not received treatment. The term "adults molested as children," (AMAC) is used in much of the literature but will not be used here because of the vagueness of the term "molestation." "Adult survivors" is used to describe both in-home and out-of-home childhood experiences.

The recent increased focus has produced new information and research about or with adult survivors. Some studies focus on research and analysis (Finkelhor, 1984; Herman, 1981; Rush, 1980; Russell, 1986; Bass & Davis, 1988), others focus on survival (Bear, 1988; Lew, 1988), and others feature survivors speaking out (Bass & Davis, 1988; Bass & Thornton, 1983; Brady, 1979; McNaron & Morgan, 1982; Morris, 1982; Fraser, 1988). These studies provide a valuable addition to our knowledge and also emphasize the currency of the information. This is certainly an issue that is with us *now*!

Presenting Problems

Although the four types of groups noted above may be doing most of the work with adult survivors, the female survivor (notes on the male survivor later) is likely to seek help initially from a counselor or other helping system. It is essential that the mental health counselor, college student counselor, or sex therapist ask questions having to do with sexual abuse. Those questions may be the turning point in the life of a survivor.

The survivor will seek help, more often than not, with the following types of presenting problems:

- depression: feelings of vulnerability, hopelessness, poor self-esteem, unclear identity;
- eating disorders: obesity, anorexia, bulimia, body image problems;
- sexual problems: dysfunction, lack of desire, addictive/compulsive patterns, anorgasmia; dystonic homosexuality;
- dissociative patterns: "spacing-out," fear of loss of reality contact, delusions, isolation; there may also be a vague feeling that something has happened but the specific memories cannot be accessed;
- somatic concerns: loss of feeling, chronic pain, gastrointestinal distress, recurrent gynecological concerns; and
- interpersonal problems: relationships, intimacy and closeness, social isolation, work/career instability.

Although this list is not exhaustive nor unique to the survivor, it helps to build an awareness of the kinds of issues that can take the form of presenting problems. It takes only a few minutes during an evaluation or initial session to ask about any sexual contact as a child.

Confronting the Issue

Once the right questions have been asked, the survivor can be encouraged to explore and confront the issue of the abuse. This is a difficult decision for survivors to make. Even though we on the outside value self-exploration and insight, the survivor may be exposing herself to great pain with only a hope that it will produce positive results eventually. Precautions related to suicide should be taken.

The counselor not only has to provide major doses of encouragement but suggest multiple options. For example, details could be discussed all at once or over a period of time, relaxation techniques or hypnotherapy could be used, names could be omitted or changed, a female therapist or co-therapist could be used, or a support person could accompany the survivor to the session(s). Once these options are discussed, the survivor should make a firm commitment to go through with this phase. If such an agreement is not made, there is a good chance that the client will not return because of the fears involved.

The disclosure itself should be made at the client's pace and in her own words. In some cases, many facts may have been repressed and as therapeutic work continues, recall may occur with accompanying intense psychological pain. The counselor can certainly clarify information as well as acknowledge feelings and should be prepared to offer support that might include more frequent therapy sessions for a limited time. Encouragement can entail recognizing the uniqueness of a client's experience as well as the commonalities with other survivors. Caution should be used against judgmental statements ("that's disgusting," "how horrible," "they should hang the bastard"). Finally, the survivor should receive reinforcement for having told her story.

Even at this early point, the survivor should be referred to a support group. The group can provide an important sense of validation and support for continuing the process.

Clarification of Responsibility

It is critical to clarify the responsibility for the abuse as being with the offender. It seems almost obvious that the survivor would blame the offender, but this is frequently not so, and the survivor has significant guilt issues. The survivor must realize that the offender is responsible for the sexual contact, no matter what she did, said, or felt, and no matter what promises or threats were made. She is entitled to rights over her own body, and if those were violated, it is the offender's responsibility.

If helpful at this point, some of the abuse dynamics can be discussed, not so much to analyze the past but to reinforce the offender's responsibility and validate the survivor's position. The survivor, like everyone else, wants to know the "why" but will benefit more from learning the "how."

As part of the clarification process, the survivor can begin to confront the offender psychologically. This may become a recurring issue throughout and beyond the treatment process. The survivor can confront through role-playing, Gestalt work, or by writing letters or a journal. She can be encouraged to vent her feelings, although they may not surface initially. Feelings can encompass rage, fear, hurt, sadness, confusion, and ambivalence. All of these should be supported.

There is frequently a question of whether the survivor should confront the offender directly if that is physically possible. There may be some significant benefit to this in terms of closure and validation, but there are also risks that the offender will deny the contact and harm the survivor again. Clearly, this step should be taken only after careful preparation for the possible consequences and only after the psychological confrontation has been settled. This step should not be viewed as necessary for recovery.

Stabilizing

The longest phase of recovery could also be labeled as "processing," "empowering," or "healing" because it is all of these. It is partly putting the jigsaw puzzle together and partly "moving on." It is a process of grief and anger, finding the child, and self-empowerment (Bass & Davis, 1988).

Recognizing the need for grief acknowledges that a significant part or the survivor's life was lost—a part of childhood that cannot be replaced. Regardless of how "mild" or "severe" the abuse was, that loss is equally real. The survivor can grieve for the joy that was lost to pain, for the innocence that was lost to guilt, for the intimacy that was lost to exploitation, and for the love that was lost to violation. Anger and sadness is each a part of the grief and needs to be repeatedly acknowledged. Group work and writing exercises can be especially helpful in this process. Visualization techniques can also help dramatically.

"Finding the child" is a process that does not encourage living in the past or replacing the lost childhood but, rather, it attempts to recreate the child within us. The concept of taking care of self is vital here. The survivor can look at ways to nurture herself in the areas of health, career, finances, and play. While still feeling in control, she can give herself permission to relax, have fun, and use support systems.

Empowerment processes include techniques that build self-esteem, self-confidence, and a sense of positive control over one's life. These might include additional education, improved decision making, outreach to other survivors, creation of support systems, expansion of the social arena, and a positive approach to spirituality.

One specific area that needs emphasis in order to experience pleasure and positive power is sexuality. Survivors need information about healthy sexual functioning and enjoyment. Many can benefit from positive sexual messages (Barbach, 1975; Zilbergeld,

1978; Barbach, 1982). Emphasis should be on engaging in sexual contact only from a positive perspective rather than as a way to please someone else. Intimacy and communication should be encouraged.

The Male Survivor

The male survivor is like the "Stealth" Bomber—invisible to radar, revealing itself only when totally safe, and potentially, explosive. As we have noted several times, the male victim and the male survivor are not likely to report pedosexual contacts because they tend not to see them as abusive and are not likely to recognize their harmful effects. We are aware, however, of a clear increase in the number of cases that are surfacing as a result of offender retrospection and referrals to treatment programs.

Three beliefs (Johanek, 1988) distort views of male victimization:

1. "Real men" would fight or resist abuse.
2. Sexual response "shouldn't" happen.
3. Offenders are homosexual and "taint" the victim.

The male survivor has similar problems and concerns to those of the female survivor with two exceptions—homophobia and the magnification of weakness. Because male victims are typically abused by male offenders, issues of possible or potential homosexuality are typical but not always in the survivor's conscious awareness. Homophobia must be clearly and directly addressed.

The other, somewhat different, concern is that the survivor feels vulnerable and violated in a society that requires men to be powerful, strong, and in control. It is the same problem that female survivors face but with added obstacles and vilification.

The male survivor will discover that support groups are difficult to find and may choose to focus on individual counseling or more general men's groups. Issues of trust and vulnerability are obvious. Again, because of societal pressures and role expectations, the male survivor might be more likely to direct his rage toward others and engage in sexual or other acting-out behavior. Although not all men who were sexually abused as children necessarily become sexual abusers as adults, the majority of adult offenders were themselves abused. Sexual addiction/compulsion and isolation both may be possible effects. Suicidal risk is high.

Supporters of Survivors

Attention should be paid to individuals and groups who serve as supporters for both male and female survivors. They should be involved in the counseling process and be provided with information, written and verbal, about pedosexual contact, abuse, and the recovery process. The extent to which specific information is disclosed is, of course, up to the survivor.

CHAPTER 5

CASE STUDIES

One of the most productive ways to gain insight into pedo-sexual problems is to study actual cases with both typical and unique components. In workshop presentations, as compared to this book, it is easier to sprinkle examples throughout. It seemed that pre-senting the cases in a more integrated manner would be helpful here.

The cases selected are all actual cases although identities, descriptive statements (age, work, etc.), and some details of the offense have been changed to protect confidentiality without chang-ing patterns of dynamics. Cases represent "successes" and "fail-ures" in terms of treatment across a spectrum of pedosexual situations.

The cases generally are presented in a chronological format; that is, presenting problem, description of offender and family, crisis intervention, ongoing treatment including pattern analysis, empowerment, termination, and follow-up.

Case Study A
C/Adu, I, R—Dictatorial/Possessive Father

Presenting Problem

Joan, age 16, in a discussion with a friend about sexual issues, revealed that she had "had sex" with her father on many occasions. Her friend, in turn, discussed this with her mother, who reported it to Child Protective Services. Joan was interviewed at school the next day by a male investigator from CPS and a female detective from the sex crimes unit of the police department. She initially denied any sexual contact and angrily refused to talk with the investigators, demanding to know where they had received their information. The investigators requested assistance from the school counselor who was reported to have a good relationship with Joan.

The counselor focused on the positive aspects of reporting, particularly on Joan's right to her own privacy and body. Joan tearfully acknowledged that her real concern was that the father may have "had sex" with her younger sister, Beth, age 13, and she didn't feel she could talk to Beth about that.

Joan reported that she had had sexual contact with her father from the time she was 11 until the age of 14. Behavior included mutual genital stroking, fellatio, and approximately five incidents of penile-vaginal coitus. The sexual contact stopped when she refused. She also refused two subsequent suggestions. She reported that she felt disgusted but that she had never been hurt. She had not reported earlier because it hadn't felt like a "big deal" and because father had told her that her mother would be very hurt and might "divorce them." She guessed that father was "having sex" with Beth because they had been alone together more often in recent months.

The CPS/police investigation team questioned Beth at her school. She angrily reported that her father had stroked her genital area through her underwear on three occasions in the last 2 months, and a week ago had coerced her into fellatio. Beth said that this made her sick (literally) but that she was afraid of reporting because her father might hurt her. She also reported that she had seen her sister and father "making love" (coitus).

Investigators interviewed the mother, Carol, who said that she believed the stories and said that she had suspected some problem but "not this." She agreed to protect the girls and to cooperate with their father's removal from the home. The girls were brought home.

The father, Dave, was questioned at work at a construction site. He denied the allegations and angrily told the investigators to mind their own business. He became agitated, was placed under arrest, and transported to the county jail. The next morning he agreed to make a statement and admitted that the allegations were correct. He was released, escorted home to pick up personal belongings, and transported to a friend's house. He was ordered to have no contact with his children.

Descriptive Information

Dave, age 37, is a construction worker (carpenter) and Carol, age 32, is a waitress. They have been married for 14 years and have three children: Joan (16), Beth (13), and Roger (9). They have lived in this community for 2 years, after having moved four times in order to obtain employment. Dave was in the army for a year and received a general discharge after two AWOL incidents. He has no criminal record but has had two convictions for driving while intoxicated. Carol has worked outside the home for most of their marriage. The children generally have performed satisfactorily at school. There had been no previous reports to Child Protective Services.

Crisis Intervention

Beth, Joan, and Carol were referred to one counselor and Dave was referred to another. Dave was arraigned and released on his own recognizance.

Beth and Joan were seen individually and each was also seen together with Carol. Beth was angry with her father, saying that she was glad to have him out of the home. She expressed fear that he would retaliate for the report and wanted to know what would happen to him. She was reassured of protection by her mother and the counselor. Her mother was able to accept Beth's anger.

Joan indicated that she didn't want to talk about the abuse and that she was sorry that she had made the report. She said that she did not feel at risk and that Beth could have stopped the contacts by refusing to participate. She also refused to talk with her mother about the report, telling her to "listen to the tape" of the investigation interview. She reluctantly agreed to continue counseling.

Dave was seen individually by his counselor. He admitted the sexual contacts although he did not think they were as frequent as Joan had reported. He said that he loved his children and that they enjoyed the sexual contact. He said that Joan had initiated several of the fellatio incidents by saying that she wanted to "make him feel good." He didn't understand why Joan wanted to stop. He also discounted Beth's reluctance, saying that she would have "liked it better when she did it more." Generally, he consistently emphasized that the children were "*his* children" and that nobody had the right to interfere with his family. He agreed to continue the counseling process and signed a suicide and treatment contract.

During subsequent crisis sessions, Joan was increasingly able to discuss her anger with her father and acknowledge that he was responsible for the behavior even though she had sometimes enjoyed "feeling like a woman." She remained reluctant to discuss specific details of the abuse but was able to discuss general issues with the counselor and with her mother.

Beth continued to be angry but shifted from never wanting to see her father to never wanting to "have him touch" her. She did not want him to go to prison because then the family "would be poor." She reported liking counseling because it was the first time that she felt she could talk about herself and her own problems.

Dave increasingly accepted responsibility for the sexual contacts even if there was a false consensuality on Joan's part. He was able to develop some trust in the counselor. He denied memories of victimization by sexual abuse, but he reported a history of physical abuse from both his parents. He was able to recognize that his father had had a similar possessiveness over his family members. At this point, Dave still had some difficulty seeing the general problem with his behavior, although he began to acknowledge the harm created by the pedosexual contact. He also acknowledged drinking about six beers a day although he denied being "an alcoholic." Throughout the crisis stage, he adhered to the restrictions imposed regarding no contact with the children. He was formally charged with two counts of attempted sexual conduct with a minor under 15. Partly because neither Beth nor Joan were willing to testify in a trial, a plea bargain was arranged and Dave was sentenced to 7 years' probation.

Carol was seen individually during the crisis phase, with frequent sessions with the children and with Dave. She expressed a great deal of anger toward Dave and discussed the possibility of divorce. When she directed this anger at him in person, he accepted it with some minimization. Carol expressed guilt over not being a satisfactory lover, but was told by Dave that their sexual relationship was not a causative factor.

The first apology sessions ended the crisis phase, approximately 3 months after the report. After preparation of and agreement from both children, separate sessions were scheduled for Joan and Beth with Carol and Dave. Joan remained passive and generally silent throughout the session, accepting Dave's apology and acknowledgment of responsibility with minimal expression of feelings. At the end of the session, she asked, "Is that it?" Beth, on the other hand, was agitated throughout her session, pressing for reasons as to why Dave "did it." She expressed anger that he "screwed up" the whole family. She wanted to know details of Dave's contacts with Joan, which were supplied.

Ongoing Treatment

During the next 7 months of treatment, Joan was seen in individual treatment, group therapy, dyad work with her mother and with Beth, and triad and family apology sessions. In the individual sessions, Joan became more at ease and openly discussed the details of the abuse. She reported being initially afraid and confused over the genital touching but agreed that after a few months, she enjoyed the "special" attention, affection, and sexual arousal. Her father had told her that she was going to experience "being a full woman" and she welcomed the coitus when he first attempted it. She reported enjoying both the sexual arousal and the feeling of "pleasing him," although she became more concerned about the possibility of pregnancy and more interested in "other" boyfriends. She became more disgusted with the sexual contact and felt that Dave was taking advantage of her.

During treatment, Joan gradually acknowledged Dave's full responsibility for the sexual contact. She remained somewhat defensive in the dyad sessions with Beth, however, because she felt that she had set up the pattern. Beth assisted this process by clearly identifying that she was angry with Dave and not Joan. Joan's dyad sessions with Carol were initially very tense until Carol expressed her feelings of resentment and even jealously toward Joan, after which Joan laughingly acknowledged the same feelings toward Carol. From that point on, Joan and Carol felt closer and began a re-bonding process.

Triad apology sessions (Joan, Carol, and Dave) continued to focus on Dave's responsibility for the sexual contact but also dealt with his general possessiveness and control over the family. Both women confronted Dave about his exploitive behavior. This theme also surfaced during the family apology sessions, with the counselor suggesting options for alternative family communication and decision making. The family sessions also addressed Roger's confusion and clarified the nature of the sexual incidents for him. Roger seemed torn between a loyalty to Dave and Carol, feeling that Dave was "mean" but that "the girls picked on him" during sessions.

Joan also attended an adolescent survivors' group. Initially, she was rather passive and was clearly reticent to discuss any facts or feelings about the abuse. It was not until several months had gone by, when she heard a story similar to hers, that she was able to identify and discuss her experiences openly. She then began to identify common experiences with other group members—trust issues, power struggles, and ambivalence. She gradually became one of the most productive and supportive members of the group.

In a parallel timeframe, Beth was seen in individual sessions, group therapy, dyad sessions with Joan and her mother, and triad and family apology sessions. In the individual sessions, Beth was able to express her anger toward both parents—anger toward her father for the abuse and generally being "mean," and anger toward her mother for "allowing" father to "be like that" and not divorcing him. She worked on somewhat typical birth-order issues like feeling "left out" or different and not receiving attention like either Joan or Roger. The counselor was able to focus effectively on the positive aspects of "being different": independence, peer relations, and assertiveness. Beth was also able to use the female counselor as a role model and develop skills in dealing with adults, resulting in improved school performance.

Beth was able to express her anger directly to Carol in their dyad sessions. Carol acknowledged her ambivalence and the consideration of divorce, but indicated that her current decision was to stay married and work on the problems. The counselor facilitated communication by modeling listening techniques for Carol. These dyad sessions seemed to produce more feelings than any of the other combinations. The triad sessions with Beth, Carol, and Dave likewise produced considerable emotional discussion, with anger, sadness, remorse, resentment, and bitterness surfacing at various times. Beth seemed to act as a catalyst for Carol's expression of feelings toward Dave.

Beth participated in a young adolescent group. In contrast to Joan, she was quickly able to open up with the group and discuss both her *and* Joan's experiences. She even became disruptive to the group process because of sexually explicit language and profanity and general limit-testing behavior. She became adept at confronting other group members in a productive way.

Carol was seen in individual treatment as well as the previously mentioned dyad, triad, and family sessions. She was also seen in marital dyad sessions. Carol initially presented as an articulate, powerful woman who, however, remained in a dependent position in relationships. She perceived that she had "no choice" but to stay in her marriage to Dave because he was the sole financial support and she did not want to "destroy the family."

Carol's family of origin was discussed. Carol is the oldest of three children. She denied a history of sexual or physical abuse. Her parents divorced when she was 9 years old and her mother worked full-time, placing Carol in the role of "assistant mother," a role she retained until she married Dave at age 17. She described the marriage as having met her expectations, which, in retrospect, she sees as low. She thought that the biggest problems were Dave's communicating only when he had demands and his alcohol consumption. Carol thought that initially the alcohol "mellowed" Dave and made him less demanding, but then it seemed to exacerbate his irresponsibility and verbal abuse.

By the end of the treatment phase, Carol had decided not to divorce Dave but felt comfortable that this was a clear choice rather than an inevitability. She was cleary placing herself in the "protector" role, with marital progress contingent on the safety of the children. Marital sessions focused on a more equitable distribution of power in the relationship and, as a part of that, improved communication. Slow progress was made on these issues with Dave willing to acknowledge Carol's strengths and the possibility that she did not have to be dependent on him. He was less willing to see himself as demanding, noting that he saw himself as inferior to Carol in many ways. It was not until late in treatment that he was able to see both of these working together (demands and inferiority feelings). Dave had a much more difficult time listening to Carol than she to him, and showed much defensiveness. Carol reported, however, that she felt that Dave heard her more consistently and thoroughly than at any time in their relationship. She reported an ease in expressing her needs, even when Dave did not fulfill them.

Carol also participated in a women's group. After an initial period of reluctance, which she attributed to lack of confidence, Carol contributed consistently to the group. She contributed both by describing her own experiences as well as by her support of other group members. She particularly befriended one member of the group. The group experience was a major vehicle in helping Carol resolve the pull between Dave and the children and also in improving her self-confidence and related assertiveness skills.

Dave's response to treatment was slow but consistent. A working diagnosis of passive-aggressive personality disorder was established. Dave adhered to the conditions of probation, although he consistently spoke about his restrictions and "the system" with hostility. With the cooperation of the probation department, he was not mandated to be free of alcohol, giving him the opportunity to stop drinking voluntarily, which he successfully accomplished. Whenever possible, Dave was given choices such as this in order to improve his sense of appropriate control and to reinforce active rather than passive responses. He remained consistently aware of his responsibility for the sexual contact.

In reviewing Dave's family of origin, he described his family as being "large and close." He was the fourth of seven children raised in a rural setting. He remembers clear expectations and rules in the family with his father in a strong authoritarian role. He described significant corporal punishment that could well be described as abusive. He also described his father as a "heavy drinker." He noted that he had always said that he respected his father but that he realized that he really "hated him." Dave became significantly remorseful when he identified his behavior with his father's, with concern that his children hated him.

It was not until over a year in treatment that Dave acknowledged his own victimization. During discussion of his sex history, specifically focusing on control versus consensus issues, Dave became silent and tearful. He reported that he had been anally raped by an uncle at 9 years of age while on a camping trip. He had not reported the abuse earlier because he felt "ashamed" and felt that it "wouldn't do any good—it's not an excuse." He was upset at himself for crying, saying that he had not cried since that abuse incident. The next several sessions dealt with his vulnerability, "macho" defenses, homophobia, and the keeping of "the secret," including the corresponding issue of acceptance of authority. He also role-played confrontation with the uncle (who is deceased). He cried several times during these follow-up sessions. He also cried during one family apology session and received support from the rest of the family.

Dave concurrently attended a men's group. For the first several months in the group, Dave presented either of two behavior patterns—passive, silent, and marginally responsive, or hostile toward "the system." He verbally pursued any situation in which Child Protective Services, law enforcement, the county attorney, or probation department was "out to screw" the average family, whether it involved his family or another. Several weeks after he accepted responsibility in individual therapy, he still refused to acknowledge fully the same responsibility in the group because it was "none of their business." As the group continued, with some "encouragement" from the probation officer regarding his need to cooperate, Dave acknowledged his responsibility and reluctantly discussed the details of his offense. He retained some verbal hostility regarding "the system" for about 6 months although he actually continued to cooperate. By the time he acknowledged his own victimization in individual therapy, he was trusting enough to also discuss it in the group at the next opportunity. He noted that the support of the group was an important "permission statement" for him. He did not cry in the group despite receiving specific permission.

Empowerment

The empowerment process for this family focused on:

1. increased focus on marriage and family sessions and more frequent visitation;
2. improved socialization; and
3. leadership in self-help and group activities.

More frequent marriage and family sessions began even while Dave was continuing his individual sessions. The major focus was on communication, problem solving, parenting skills, and appropriate individuation. Of these tasks, communication remained difficult if more than a triad (of any combination) was present. There seemed to be increased competition for attention and increased defensiveness. This continued as a moderate problem area through reunification. The other tasks were accomplished by using subsystems of the family. Each member of the family became stronger individually.

Marital therapy also included sexuality issues, specifically enrichment and consensus. With the assistance of a sexuality class, Dave and Carol were able to get more information regarding options for their sexual behavior. In particular, they reported pleasure from increased nongenital touching, including stroking and massage. Carol also became comfortable in initiating sexual contact, which both she and Dave saw as positive.

Once the apology sessions were under way, the visitation process began. The family began with supervised public visitation, then home visits of increasing duration. After some initial discomfort expressed by both Dave and Beth, the visits seemed to be an important bonding force. The family reported that it was the first time they consistently had fun together. After gradual increases in time together, overnight visits were introduced, were carefully monitored, and were seen as successful.

Individually, as a couple, and as a family, there was a clear increase in the amount of socialization (and therefore, decrease in isolative behavior). The parents became good friends with a couple from their therapy group and, for the first time in their married life, engaged in social activities with this couple (movies, football games, etc.). The children, particularly Joan and Roger, enlarged their circle of friends both through the treatment program and at school. Both Beth's and Roger's school performance improved.

Within the self-help component of treatment, Dave, Carol, and Joan all assumed leadership positions. Carol was elected vice-president of the self-help group and acted as a sponsor for three women new to the program. Dave coordinated the group's support program, assisting other families with home repairs, vehicle repairs, and a food and clothing bank. Joan was elected president of the children's component and organized several new activities.

Termination

After approximately 2 years in the treatment program, the family was reviewed for reunification. Dave underwent an independent reevaluation by court personnel, who saw him as significantly improved but still retaining some passive-aggressive features. Recommendations were made for continued treatment after reunification. The family met with the treatment team to clarify and review comfort levels, protection strategies, and relapse prevention. The family committed to continued treatment. The treatment team approved their reunification, with the judge lifting restrictions on contact and visitation.

The family continued in treatment for 6 months after reunification. The children and Carol terminated their individual therapy after monitoring of the effects of reunification. This monitoring was also the focus of Dave's individual sessions and conjoint family sessions. After commitments were made for ongoing contacts, Dave and the family were terminated from treatment approximately 2½ years after the report of abuse.

Case Study B
C/Adu, I, R—Dependent Father

Presenting Problem

Kevin's 4th grade teacher referred him to the school counselor and nurse because of a dramatic change in behavior, including aggressive incidents toward peers almost daily and three incidents of enuresis during class. Kevin angrily denied any problems, saying that he was simply defending himself against other children and that the fighting and arguing was worse since his "accidents." A follow-up session with the counselor was approached in a more indirect, supportive manner. Kevin admitted that he was worried about his stepfather "losing his job again." Even though he liked having more time to spend with his stepfather, Kevin didn't like the fact that, in the past, it also meant that his stepfather would be "drinking beer and smoking pot." When asked what would be the worst thing about that, Kevin said that they would play "weird sex games." He said this included "touching and licking each other's weenie" and that he didn't like to do that because it felt funny. The counselor assured Kevin that he did not have to do that and that it was understandable that he didn't like it.

The school counselor reported the conversation to the school nurse, principal, and Child Protective Services. An investigative team from CPS/police arrived later that day. After an introduction from the counselor, Kevin discussed the sexual contacts with the investigators. He reported three incidents of mutal penile stroking and fellatio during the previous 6 months. In each case, the step-father initiated contact "when he was pretty drunk." All three incidents happened while his mother was at work. There was apparently no ejaculation or attempt at anal penetration. Kevin had been told that it would be "our secret" but his stepfather exerted no overt threats or force.

The investigators interviewed both Kevin's mother, Karen, and stepfather, Danny, at home. Danny admitted to two incidents as alleged by Kevin but didn't remember a third. He stated that he felt ashamed and worthless and that he had been depressed and drinking excessively, having lost 3 jobs in the last year. Karen was extremely angry, initially wanting him arrested but then wanting him "locked up in the hospital." She indicated that he had talked about suicide on several occasions and that she didn't want him to do that. He acknowledged suicidal ideation, past and current. He was taken into custody and placed in the mental health unit of the county jail on a suicide watch. Kevin was returned home.

Descriptive Information

Danny, age 28, was unemployed at the time of the arrest, having worked as a dishwasher, short-order cook, and delivery driver. Carol, age 30, is employed as a receptionist. Carol has one child, Kevin, age 9, from a previous relationship. This is the first marriage for both. They have been married for 2 years after having lived together for 3 years. They both have lived in this community since they were children. Both have completed high school. Karen has been employed at three different clerk/receptionist jobs since graduation, leaving one because of her pregnancy. Danny has not held any job for more than a year, estimating that he has had 15 to 20 jobs. He describes himself as a "slow learner" and that he typically gets fired for "making stupid mistakes," although recently he was fired from two jobs for smoking marijuana on the job. He has no criminal history. Kevin is a 4th-grade student who had been receiving excellent grades up until the last 6 months prior to the report. There have been no previous reports to Child Protective Services.

Crisis Intervention

Danny was arraigned and released from jail in 5 days after two evaluations by the jail consulting psychiatrist. He moved into a trailer. He was immediately assigned to a counselor and a sponsor from the self-help organization. He acknowledged his continuing depression, guilt, and shame but denied further suicidal ideation, saying that "getting caught was the best thing that ever happened to me." He agreed to a suicide contract and an abstinence agreement, saying that drinking and marijuana use were the cause of all his problems. (As a condition of release, he was also required to submit to urinalysis twice a week.) Although the counselor supported Danny's decision to abstain, he also confronted Danny with his simplistic answer. Because Danny reported that he felt dependent on his daily marijuana use more so than on alcohol, he was also referred to Narcotics Anonymous and began attending daily groups. He was formally arrested and agreed to a plea bargain of a guilty plea to one count of attempted sexual conduct with a minor. He was sentenced to 7 years probation, 1 year in the county jail work release program, and mandatory abstinence from alcohol and other drugs. He began work as a short-order cook and began serving his jail sentence, with release time for work and therapy.

Karen was assigned to an individual counselor and crisis group. She remained angry at Danny but hoped that the report and arrest would "straighten him up." She expressed guilt that she frequently joined him in his marijuana use, although she denied any knowledge or suspicion of the pedosexual contact. She described the marital relationship as good except for Danny's "irresponsibility." She generally described their sexual relationship as "very exciting and active," but lately she had been concerned that their sexual activity depended on their use of marijuana as a relaxant. She expressed considerable concern about her choice of "losers" in relationships but did not express any intention of divorcing Danny. Although prior to this incident Karen had not seen her marijuana use as harmful, she agreed to voluntary abstinence. She clearly seemed supportive and protective of Kevin.

Kevin was seen by an individual counselor, with a focus on play therapy and expression of feelings. He verbally and nonverbally expressed anger toward Danny but hoped he would "get help." He was kept informed of the criminal justice process. He expressed hope that the family could get back together after Danny got "fixed" and was given support that he would be safe. Kevin had told his friends that Danny was "in trouble for drugs," therefore avoiding dealing with the sexual issue. Generally, he seemed to be able to "take care of himself." He continued to see the sexual behavior as "weird" and was worried that Danny might have done something that hurt, although he denied any physical pain (or pleasure) from the contacts. After preparation, apology sessions were held with Kevin, Karen, and Danny, and the counselors involved. Danny tearfully apologized and accepted responsibility for the three incidents. He cried throughout the first apology session. He positively reinforced the report, saying that he was "proud" of Kevin. Kevin remained passive during the first two apology sessions, accepting and understanding Danny's verbalizations but not showing any affective response. He quickly agreed with the counselors' suggestions that he was still afraid. Both parents spontaneously supported his fear as being "OK." By the third apology session, he initiated hugging Danny but still remained somewhat passive affectively.

Just as the decision to allow family visitation at the jail was being considered, Danny tested positive for marijuana use in a routine screen. A subsequent search revealed two marijuana "joints" in his locker. His work release and visitation privileges were cancelled for 90 days, and counseling sessions were held at the jail. At the end of the 90 days, another apology session was held so that the family could deal with this setback. Both Kevin and Karen expressed their anger at Danny.

Ongoing Treatment

Danny was seen in individual, group, marital, and family sessions as well as Narcotics Anonymous. Individual sessions focused on responsibility issues (general, drug-related, and sexual), positive control, and self-esteem. Working diagnoses were dysthymic disorder and dependent personality disorder.

A review of Danny's history showed that he is the youngest of three children from an intact family. He remembered his childhood as being "very normal" with no major problems. He denied abuse. He reported moderate alcohol use by his father. He described consistent problems in school, having been retained in one elementary grade and then dropping out of high school in the 9th grade. He reported starting to use marijuana at that time, quickly becoming a regular user. He started drinking beer at age 18 but continued to prefer marijuana. He denied other drug use.

Danny described his sexual history as "frustrating" prior to his marriage. He reported consistent masturbation and two or three heterosexual contacts. Further exploration of the masturbation patterns yielded a sense of addiction, at least during his early adulthood. Danny reported that he would sometimes masturbate five times a day and that he frequently experienced penile irritation. He denied homosexual contacts. He remembered severe self-esteem problems due to his inability to attract or maintain sexual partners. He connects this with a significant fear of loss of his relationship with Karen, with whom he has had a "wonderful" sexual relationship.

Treatment strategies of supportive confrontation related to issues of self-control, responsibility, and personal power. Control was improved with consistent monitoring for further drug use and through the "12-step" Narcotics Anonymous program. General control was improved, with assumption of control over progressively more complex decisions. Power and responsibility were likewise increased, with positive emphasis on his job. Assertiveness skills were addressed. The incarceration in the county jail seemed to add a sense of structure to Danny's life that he had previously lacked. Although he reported "hating" his time there, he had functioned on a more consistent basis and seemed to have improved motivation.

Marital dyad sessions focused on power sharing. This became particularly important as Karen became stronger and more assertive regarding her needs. Communication was initially very basic, with considerable emphasis on affective awareness. Dynamics of dependency and codependency on each other and marijuana received special emphasis. The sexual relationship was viewed both for its positives as well as its contribution to the dependency problems.

Parenting issues and skills were addressed in both marital and family sessions. Kevin seemed to engage in frequent power struggles with both parents, testing limits particularly regarding bedtime and responsibilities (chores). By eventually handling these struggles, both parents were able to improve their self-esteem and Kevin seemed more secure.

Danny's group also provided important supportive confrontation. Responsibility issues were consistently addressed by group members, who identified with each other. Danny's drug issues seemed to be unique to the group but other members seemed to translate the issues to their own dependency problems. Danny participated more in group but remained somewhat passive.

Karen was also seen in individual, marital, family, and group sessions. Individual sessions focused on her dependency issues and ways for her to feel more powerful and in control of her own life. Decision-making skills were emphasized. Karen's history showed several areas of strength—positive school history, apparently normal family background, and skills in dealing with people. As she had indicated earlier, however, she did not feel confident in her relationships with men. She had engaged in several relationships beginning in high school with similar results—dating would lead to a sexual relationship and then the relationship would end. She had felt used and dissatisfied until she began dating Danny. Because Danny seemed less demanding, she felt more comfortable, feeling that they could "take care of each other." She intially saw their mutual use of marijuana as a bond, preferring it to the possibility of Danny going off on his own to drink or smoke (which he had, in fact, also been doing).

After several months in treatment, Karen admitted that she had not felt as satisfied with the sexual relationship as she had originally stated. Although she appreciated Danny's affection and his finding her attractive, she saw the contacts as increasingly repetitious and dependent on the marijuana for arousal. Danny consistently seemed to demand fellatio as his means of satisfaction, with decreasing concern for her needs. As noted, this became a major focus in the marital sessions.

Group sessions seemed to be particularly helpful for Karen. She gained support from identifying with the other group members and improved her self-esteem through comments from the group about her strengths, attractiveness, and competence. The group also became a resource for parenting issues.

Kevin was seen in individual and family sessions. He participated briefly in a play therapy group but was seen as too mature for the young children's group. At the time, there were not enough male victims to form a separate group. Later in treatment, he became a helper in the young children's play group.

Individual sessions for Kevin focused on his feeling of being "left out" of the family and his attempts at power struggles in order to become more like the adults in the family. He was encouraged to take appropriate responsibility in the family and was praised for his school performance. He also began an after-school sports program for the first time.

Empowerment

The empowerment process focused on family communication and activities, particularly those with other families. After Danny's release from jail, family visits were scheduled with increasing duration. The visits decreased Kevin's feelings of isolation within the family because he was given an active voice in planning the activity of a particular visit. The activity focus also countered Danny's passivity and supported each of the family members' decision-making skills. Although Karen, particularly, established a network of friends within the treatment program, the family as a group became more involved with church-related activities. They had been marginally involved with church early in their marriage but had not been involved at all with the related social activities. They felt comfortable with large group activities (dinners, volleyball) and maintained contact with two of the other families in between activities.

Partially because of the setback in treatment due to Danny's marijuana use and partially because of the treatment teams' concern about possible relapse, the family remained in the treatment program longer than most families. Although this engendered some frustration, the family also became better able to advocate for itself and, yet, accept the limits imposed by society. Danny, particularly, was able to speak assertively, but with control, with members of the treatment team.

Termination

Almost 3 years after the report, the treatment team approved reunification for the family. The family continued in treatment as a unit for 4 months after that. Danny was mandated to continue attendance at Narcotics Anonymous and required to submit to random urinalyses for the duration of his probation.

Approximately a year after termination, Karen and Danny returned for four sessions of marital therapy to deal with his termination from employment. These sessions focused on his self-esteem and her concerns about Danny's repeating old patterns. These issues seemed to have been resolved, Danny obtained new employment, and there did not seem to be any new concerns.

Case Study C
Ado/Adu, I, R—Pseudoadult Child

Presenting Problem

Marianne, age 17, requested a pregnancy test from her family physician, fearing that she was pregnant as a result of sexual intercourse with her father. She disclosed one incident of penile-vaginal penetration with ejaculation, and multiple incidents of genital stroking, fellatio, and cunnilingus. The pregnancy test was negative. After discussion with Marianne, the physician reported the information to Child Protective Services.

Marianne disclosed the same information to the investigators, saying that she and her father had been "having an affair" for the last 6 to 7 months that included progressively more overt sexual behavior, almost on a daily basis. She guessed that there were at least 20 incidents of cunnilingus. She confirmed only one coital contact, occurring 3 weeks before the report. She denied any violence or threats, saying that she was willing to do "the other things" even though she didn't like it, but that she was afraid of getting pregnant or contracting AIDS if he continued to "make love to me." She reported that she had refused a subsequent advance by the father and he had not approached her for the 2 weeks prior to the report. She said that she didn't want to get him in trouble if he would stop.

Because there was no mother in the home, Marianne and her younger brother, James (12), were placed in their (paternal) grandparents' home after it was determined that this would be a safe environment. The investigators interviewed the father, Tom, who admitted the contacts and said that he was "waiting for something to happen after I went too far." Tom was arrested and released to his own custody after agreeing to have no contact with the children nor with his parents, nor to visit their home.

Descriptive Information

Tom, age 36, is a landscape foreman, having worked with this company for approximately 7 years. He has been a single parent since his wife, Mary, left the family 10 years before. None of the family has had contact with Mary since that time and they presume she is living in another state. Both Tom and Marianne described Mary as "nice but flaky" and "stressed-out" by the demands of parenting. Tom reports no significant relationships since Mary left because he "didn't have time" and "didn't feel comfortable" around women.

Marianne, 17, is a junior in high school. She reports average grades but limited extracurricular activity because she has always "taken care of" her brother and father. This includes cooking, housecleaning, and most of the laundry. She remembers "watching" her brother essentially since her mother left. She took over most of the cooking at age 11. She denies any particular relationship with a boyfriend although indicates that she has lots of friends at school.

James, 12, is a 5th-grade student who had been retained in first grade. He receives fair to poor grades but is described by teachers as a "hard worker." He denied any knowledge of the sexual contact between his father and sister. He also denied any contact between him and his father.

The family all described themselves as "close" and used to working "as a team." They reported frequent contact with the father's parents and with the father's sister and her family who also live in the community.

Crisis Intervention

Child Protective Services filed a dependency petition and were granted legal custody of Marianne and James, physical custody remaining with the grandparents. All parties agreed to a plan for foster placement with the aunt and uncle after their home was reviewed and licensed as a foster home.

After learning of the possible prison sentence that her father faced, Marianne recanted her story, saying that she had been angry at her father and that she had really "had sex" with a boyfriend, whom she refused to identify. Because of this recantation, the lack of physical evidence, and inadmissibility of the father's "confession" because of civil rights ("Miranda") procedural errors, the county attorney dismissed the criminal charges against Tom. The dependency, however, continued in force, including the "no-contact" provisions.

Tom voluntarily agreed to treatment, regardless of the dismissal, with the hopes of reuniting the family. He was assigned an individual counselor but declined group treatment because he feared he might incriminate himself. He was fully cooperative with the individual counselor and quickly developed a trusting relationship. Crisis issues included suicide prevention and focus on regaining control over his life. Initially extremely guilty and depressed over the loss of his children, he came to see the opportunity to "regroup" and build a new relationship once the charges were dismissed. Because he did not have a spouse or significant other, a crisis support team was established by scheduling counseling twice a week and involving two of his work colleagues. During the "no-contact" period, his counselor maintained contact with the children's counselor in order to reassure Tom of their progress.

Marianne was assigned to an individual counselor and support group. She refused to talk directly about her report on the allegations against her father but agreed to "listen." In both settings, she received support for both the report and the recantation, with messages that each was reasonable and a way to take care of herself. She was given permission to discuss more general issues, including her feelings about being placed in the pseudoadult role and related issues of her loss of childhood. She responded positively to this permission and actively participated in both modalities.

James was assigned to the same counselor as Marianne. He indicated that he believed Marianne's initial report but that he still wanted the family to "get help" and get back together. He seemed to make a good adjustment to living with the grandparents, who he felt were also supportive of reuniting the original family. He reluctantly expressed anger toward his father. He did "not exactly" see Marianne as being in a maternal role but did agree that he was dependent on her.

Ongoing Treatment

Tom continued in individual treatment. Goals included a more balanced, controlled approach to parenting and caring for himself, including increased socialization and active, positive planning and decision making. Redirection of sexual outlets was also clearly a major goal.

Tom's history indicated that he is the younger of two children with his family of origin still in close contact. He reported a lifelong history of obesity to a greater or lesser degree and related peer problems with name-calling and rejection. He also reported a negative body image and very poor self-esteem, leading to suicidal ideation during adolescence. He had not made any suicidal gestures and denied further ideation. He saw his wife, Mary, as somebody who "felt sorry for me" and "liked me because I was loyal and dependable, like a puppy dog." He described the marriage as good for a few years with a sexual relationship that felt good for Tom but never seemed to satisfy Mary completely. He felt that the birth of James was a last effort to save the marriage and that he was surprised that Mary left him to care for the children. He described the children as the "only thing I've got" and saw the relationship with Marianne as "always affectionate." He acknowledged his responsibility for the sexual contact as well as the more general responsibility for placing her in the pseudoadult role. His sex history had been limited to masturbation and occasional (once or twice a year) visits to prostitutes since his divorce. He denied sexual arousal by children and reported fantasies of women finding him attractive. At the time of treatment, he was moderately overweight but had good muscle tone. Working diagnoses were dependent personality disorder and major chronic depression.

Treatment strategies included reinforcing positive decision making and creating options rather than adhering to his previously rigid style. Tom was encouraged to pursue socialization with women, which resulted in several "dates" and dramatically improved his self-image. He was invited to create controlled fantasies regarding some of these women.

Apology sessions were held initially with Marianne and later with both Marianne and James. Tom tearfully apologized to both children and accepted responsibility for both general and sex-specific issues. Marianne confronted him with feelings of anger, focusing on the sense of the loss of her childhood.

Marianne's individual and group sessions were accelerated because of the limited timeframe of the dependency petition. She was able to identify feelings of anger and ambivalence and, most clearly, loss of both her mother and her own childhood. She became able to define appropriate roles and tasks for herself and redefine her relationship with James as a result of the placement with the grandparents and, later, with the aunt and uncle. She developed a close relationship with a boy at school and began dating.

Family visits began early in the treatment process, shortly after the apology sessions. Initially, visits were supervised by the aunt but became unsupervised 2 months before Marianne's 18th birthday. Marianne reported positive feelings of comfort during the visits, noting that both she and her father had changed. These visits and family counseling sessions focused on planning appropriate roles in the family and setting up support systems (friends and extended family) and protection mechanisms (locks on bedroom and bathroom doors, family discussions).

Termination

The dependency status of both children was dropped on Marianne's 18th birthday. With the lifting of restrictions, the family reunited after an accelerated treatment program of 7 months. The family voluntarily continued treatment for 3 months of family sessions and then terminated.

A one-year follow-up indicated that Marianne was preparing to be married in the near future and would be leaving the state with her new husband. Tom acknowledged mixed feelings about the marriage but thought, overall, that it would be good. He reported continued dating but "nothing serious," and an occasional sexual contact with one of these dates. James was continuing to struggle in school. An invitation to return to counseling was turned down.

Case Study D
C/Adu, E, P—Pedophile

Presenting Problem

Norman, age 26, was referred by a clergyman after an allegation of sexual conduct with a 4-year-old child had been investigated and deemed unsubstantiated. Norman had expressed concerns regarding his sexuality to the clergyman, who referred him for specialized treatment.

At his initial appointment, Norman seemed to be extremely anxious and tearfully described his problem by saying, "I love children. I *really* love children." He reported that he was extremely frightened about the investigation and the possibility of going to prison. Without specifically acknowledging his responsibility for the pedosexual contact, he described himself as a "sick man" who desperately needed help.

Descriptive Information

Norman is a clerk-typist employed in a large real estate business. He currently lives with his mother because of financial difficulties but has lived on his own during two periods of his life for as long as 2 years. He is a high school graduate with one year of community college credit. He has been employed by three different firms since high school graduation, having left the two previous firms because he felt like he "wasn't getting anywhere." He reports similar dissatisfaction with his current job. He describes himself as a "hermit" who only wants to be involved in activities that include children.

Crisis Intervention

The major focus of the crisis phase was suicide prevention. In the initial session, Norman described himself as worthless and "the lowest of the low" and said that he had considered taking "an overdose of something" but hadn't acted on it. He refused a recommendation for voluntary hospitalization but agreed to a suicide contract and telephone contact between sessions. After discussions with Norman, the counselor also confirmed with his mother that she was available to him for support and that she would report any concerns or problems. Norman was only willing to acknowledge to his mother that he was depressed and would not acknowledge any of the sexual issues.

Ongoing Treatment

Norman remained in treatment for 2 years, with goals of redirecting his sexual preference and generally reducing his dependence on children. It became apparent that Norman had actually engaged in sexual contact on one occasion, that being an incident of his touching the genitals of the aforementioned 4-year-old boy. He has, however, had a long-term obsession with children with sexual arousal by young (prepubertal) boys. He described, in a rather child-like manner, his desire to play with children, teach them, and hug and kiss them, most of the time without sexual arousal. He described himself as a "Pied Piper" in that children seemed spontaneously at ease and playful with him. He would frequently take friends' children to the park, zoo, or other activities and was regarded as "the best babysitter of all time."

Norman is an only child, having been reared by his mother after an early divorce. He does not remember any contact with his father. He described himself as a "sissy" child in that he was frequently picked on at school for his somewhat meek behavior and his eyeglasses. He had seen himself as an awkward and clumsy child. Although he denied any pedosexual contact with an adult, he remembered several incidents of sex play with other boys, including mutual genital stroking and fellatio. Between this and a lack of interest in girls in high school, he had assumed he was gay but did not take any action on that belief. After high school graduation, he began to date girls and was surprised to find himself enjoying the experience and becoming aroused, although there was no overt sexual behavior. He also had one same-sex experience, mutual fellatio, which he found moderately arousing. Based on information that he had read, he concluded that he was bisexual but really did not find sexual contact with either men or women consistently arousing.

While in high school, Norman began babysitting. He enjoyed this and received a lot of positive comments. He remembered being curious and then, later, aroused by catching glimpses of young (3 to 5-year-old) children's genitals and set up situations where he assisted them in changing or going to the bathroom. Children younger than 5 did not seem aware of his behavior. He would indirectly contact the genitals by tickling, hugging, or wrestling. Within the last year before this referral, he began taking pictures of children in bathing suits, underwear, or nude. He denied exposing himself or having direct genital contact except for the one reported incident.

During the first 6 months of treatment, Norman refrained from any contact with children. He redirected his attention toward career concerns and toward exploring relationships with adult women. He dated two women who had young children and quickly shifted his attention to the children, which initially made him even more attractive to the women but eventually turned them off. He did not engage in sexual contact with the women. Norman interpreted these relationships as rejecting. For the duration of treatment, he made some initiatives toward women but generally felt inept, unable to converse, and uncomfortable. He had no social or friendship relationships with adult men.

Norman had some success with fantasy redirection. He was able to masturbate to fantasy themes involving women and denied similar behavior involving children. He reported being more aware about his sexual preference as being heterosexual.

Norman reported continued contact with children in supervised or controlled situations and expressed pleasure over his nonsexual contact with children. He felt most positive about his ability to relate to children and keep it nonsexual, giving him a feeling of "the best of both worlds." At one point he became rather depressed when he had not had contact with children for a week. The counselor confronted the obsessive nature of the behavior more frequently, which sometimes increased his guilt. When his contacts with children became less supervised and he reinitiated babysitting activities, he was confronted even more strongly and encouraged to alter his behavior.

Approximately 2 years after the initial referral, a 9-year-old reported that Norman had licked his penis while he was sleeping at Norman's house. Norman was arrested while holding a knife to his throat and was placed in custody at the mental health unit of the county jail. A police search revealed several photographs of children. He was convicted of sexual conduct with a minor and multiple counts of sexual exploitation (for the photographs) and is currently serving a 38-year sentence.

Case Study E
C/Adu, E, P—Pedophile

Presenting Problem

Frank, age 52, was referred for evaluation by his defense attorney. Frank had been charged with molestation of a 5-year-old friend of his granddaughter, specifically genital touching. The evaluation was requested to substantiate this contact as an isolated incident and rule out pedophilia, thereby affecting the sentencing decision.

Evaluation Summary

Frank presented as an unusually well-dressed and groomed individual. He is retired from the military and is currently in a senior management position in a computer company. He described the allegations against him and accepted the responsibility for his behavior, tearfully stating that it was a "stupid, stupid mistake" and that he had no idea why it happened. He reported that he has been asking himself "Why?" and can only think of the great stress he has been under since his recent divorce and business problems. He specifically denied any other pedosexual contacts or extraordinary interest in children.

Frank's psychosocial history was reviewed and did not yield any significant indicators of concern except for possible alcohol misuse. His sex history, likewise, seemed to indicate typical psychosexual development and arousal patterns. He reported peer contacts during adulthood with no preferred arousal to younger women. There did not seem to be any interest in sexual power and control issues. Preference had always been heterosexual with mild homophobia.

Psychological testing showed above average intelligence, strong memory and attention and a valid, normal Minnesota Multiphasic Personality Inventory (MMPI) profile. Thematic Apperception Test and Incomplete Sentences responses were descriptive and somewhat concrete but seen to be within normal limits.

Psychophysiological assessment using the plethysmograph detected consistent penile arousal to pictures of young children. When confronted with the graphic evidence, Frank admitted that he had been aroused by child pornography for "many years," particularly by photographs of nude prepubertal children. He denied other direct pedosexual contacts because of fear of incrimination. He acknowledged that he did have a "small collection" of pictures and magazines that he had destroyed after this recent report. He refused to answer whether he had taken any of these pictures.

Based on the persistence of the arousal pattern and the strong probability of other pedosexual contacts in his history, Frank was classified as a pedophile in the report submitted to the court. Because of his lack of previous convictions and exemplary military and employment record, a plea bargain was accepted that resulted in "no contest" pleas to attempted molestation and sexual exploitation. He is serving two concurrent 5-year sentences in the state prison.

Case Study F

C/Adu, I, R and Ado/Adu, I, Ra—Adolescent Survivor

Presenting Problem

Cindy, 16, was referred for counseling by the juvenile court after a second arrest for prostitution and possession of marijuana and cocaine. Previous treatment for substance abuse had apparently been only marginally effective. She has been a runaway for 2 years and her family has not been located. Sexual abuse has been suspected but Cindy has consistently denied it.

Crisis Intervention

Cindy was initially seen while still in the juvenile detention center. She was extremely hostile and resistant to counseling. She was granted her request for a female counselor. She minimized the referral problems by saying that she was not using drugs as much as she used to and that the prostitution shouldn't be against the law because "nobody gets hurt" and "it's good money." She asserted that she had been supporting herself "real good" for the last 2 years by "having sex, which everybody agrees is fun."

In order to diffuse Cindy's resistance, she was given the power to choose topics for the counseling. She chose to vent anger and hostility at "the system" for unfairly punishing her and, by the third session, began to talk about her anger and concern that a boyfriend had "dumped" her. This led to a more general discussion of problems with boys and men. In the 10th session, she was angrily stating that "all men fuck you over" when she started to cry for the first time. She sobbed that, "I really got fucked over!" She reported that her stepfather (mother's second husband) had physically abused her throughout her childhood, beating her with a belt on her bare buttocks on a weekly basis for anything she had done wrong. After he had "disciplined" her, she would have to remain nude from the waist down and bent over a chair so he could "make sure I wasn't really hurt." During one of these sessions at age 11, she peeked and noticed that he was masturbating. He invited her "for a closer look," and from that time until she was 13, replaced the weekly beating ritual by giving Cindy the "choice" of fellatio instead. Cindy finally reported this to her mother when he began forcing her to swallow his ejaculate. Mother "kicked him out of the house" but told Cindy not to tell anyone because she (mother) might get into trouble.

Continuing the history over a lengthy crisis session, Cindy reported that her mother began living with a "boyfriend" when she was 14. One evening when her mother was working the night shift, the boyfriend became drunk and woke Cindy. He threatened to beat her if she made a sound and proceeded to perform cunnilingus and then forcibly penetrate her (penile-vaginal and penile-anal). He slapped her once when she cried in pain. After he passed out, she gathered some possessions and ran away from home, spending the night in a riverbed. When she called home the next day, her mother was very angry and didn't believe her story, saying that Cindy wasn't "going to cost me another man." Her mother told her to return home immediately or "forget it." Cindy did not return home.

The crisis intervention shifted at that point to focus on Cindy's rage and lack of trust in men, with role-playing, visualization, and writing (the latter limited by Cindy's expressive language problems).

Treatment

Cindy was placed in a group foster home and was monitored for alcohol or other drug use. Individual sessions continued to focus on her rage as well as her guilt over her behavior. She felt that she had, in fact, chosen the fellatio over the physical punishment and should have instead "taken her punishment." It took several sessions before she was able to clearly see the stepfather's manipulation and sexual motivation. Likewise, for some time, she was convinced that she had done something to cause the rape because "why would two men want to do the same thing?" She dealt with similar issues in an adult survivors' group that she attended.

Six weeks after her placement in the group home, she was caught smoking marijuana. She was detained for 48 hours and placed in another group home. She again minimized the marijuana use but agreed to refrain. Treatment emphasis was shifted to focus on her own recovery regardless of the traumatic history. She seemed to stabilize and abide by the rules of the group home. School attendance became consistent. After 6 months, treatment issues were expanded to include relationships, self-esteem, rejection, and power issues. She continued to deny or minimize problems that did arise.

One year after the initial referral, Cindy ran away from the group home after being accused of sexual conduct with another girl in the home. Two years after that, there remains no evidence of her whereabouts.

Case Study G
C/Adu, E, P—Adult Survivor

Presenting Problem

Debra, age 26, self-referred with concerns about "confused feelings regarding sex." Sometimes she felt "turned on" with her boyfriend but at other times she felt repulsed, particularly when he engaged in cunnilingus in a similar manner as she had experienced during a pedosexual contact. She indicated that she had sexual contact between the ages of 5 to 7 with a neighbor who "was like another father." She had recently been reminded of this contact when she saw this man and her father cheerfully waved to him, which infuriated her. She denied other problems or concerns unrelated to these.

Descriptive Information

Debra is an assistant manager in a retail business. She is a graduate of a community college and has been employed for 6 years. She lives with her family in her childhood home although she spends as much time as possible in her boyfriend's home. She is the younger of two children, with a brother 3 years older. Her parents remain in their first marriage. She has been in her current relationship with her lover for 2 years. During that time, she describes having had a very good sexual relationship and good intimate communication. She notes that her lover is being supportive of her regarding the current issues.

Crisis Intervention

Debra described the history as she could remember it, although she reported that much of the details remained "fuzzy" because of the time lapse and because she had "tried to block it out." She remembers that her father never seemed to have time for her, so she spent a lot of time with a neighbor, John, and his daughter. During that time, roughly between the ages of 5 and 7, she remembers "games" that involved disrobing and, more clearly, genital stroking and cunnilingus. She does not remember other sexual acts although she assumes that they may have happened. She does not think there was any penetration. She remembers being uneasy and telling her parents, who did not believe her. They both emphasized that John was a friend who wouldn't hurt her and that she must have misunderstood a game or sign of affection. She insisted that they confront John and they invited him to the house for a discussion. He denied all the allegations with "smiling sincerity" and the parents believed him, although her mother did suggest not going to his house any more. Her father chastised Debra. For the rest of her childhood and adolescence she remembered being both angry and afraid. She had heard rumors that John had engaged in similar sexual games with his daughter and, later, a granddaughter and other children. Even though these were rumors, they certainly seemed to fit the pattern of a pedophile. She remembered confronting him at age 16 and asking him why he did it. He smiled and said, "Because I loved you." She continued to hate him but was able to avoid him for most of her adult life until the recent incident when she saw her father wave to him. She "blew up" at her father and, since then, has been preoccupied with anger and rage toward John, her father, and, to a lesser extent, her mother. She feels vulnerable, unsupported, and unprotected by everyone except her lover.

Debra cried throughout the discussion of the history. She said she understood the rage but didn't understand the confused feelings that she has had. Most of the first two sessions were devoted to this history, positive support, and information that her reactions were, indeed, appropriate. In the third session, she agreed to a suggestion for anger work. An "empty chair" technique was used to encourage expression of anger. She quickly "confronted" John with her hurt and anger but seemed rather controlled in doing it. She did not respond to any suggestion of striking out at him or hurting him. When confronted with her rather mild reactions and reluctance to "let him have it" verbally or physically, she stopped talking and crying for several minutes and then sobbed uncontrollably when she said that she couldn't really hurt him because she had loved him. Later in that session, she acknowledged that it was the first time she had ever dealt with the ambivalence and with the "double hurt" that comes from being violated by someone you trust and not being protected by someone who should be a protector.

Ongoing Treatment

Continuing treatment focused on ways that she could feel safe and be in positive control both within her sexual relationship and within the family. Conjoint sessions were held with her lover to discuss ways that she could better express her needs for safety. Debra and her friend were able to develop new sexual and non-sexual (stroking) patterns to reinforce their mutual control over their own pleasuring. Eventually, they were able to desensitize the cunnilingus behavior through relaxation and gradual increase in the duration of the behavior from a few seconds to several minutes to the point where Debra reported again being orgasmic with that behavior.

Regarding her family, Debra was able to ask for support regarding her *current* feelings rather than, again, introducing the debate over what had happened 20 years ago. Her mother was willing and able to be supportive and listened to Debra's feelings about the protection/vulnerability issues. Her father acknowledged her pain but refused to deal with it, insisting that she forget it and get on with her life. Presumably because of this position, her parents refused Debra's invitation to family sessions.

Debra benefited greatly from writing about her feelings and composing letters and poems to John and her parents and then, for the most part, destroying them. She also gained support from an adult survivors' group, receiving considerable validation for the feelings of rage and ambivalence/confusion.

During the 8-month treatment period, she earned a promotion at work and reported improved self-esteem, assertiveness, and sense of control over her life. She also moved in with her lover on a full-time basis.

Termination

Individual counseling was terminated after approximately 8 months. Debra reported greatly improved control and only occasional outbursts of rage regarding John. She was encouraged to continue these outbursts in a safe setting. Debra continued her involvement with the adult survivors' group for 2 years, becoming a peer facilitator during the last year. She also developed two strong friendships with women in the group. A year after termination from the group, these friends reported that she continued to be doing well.

No substantive evidence was ever gathered against John. He has never been arrested or reported for sexual abuse.

Case Study H
Ado/Adu, I, S—Female Offender

Presenting Problem

Richard, age 15, called the community information service to find out how his stepmother could be "forced into someplace to get help for her drug problem when she doesn't want to go." During the discussion, he talked about her heavy use of cocaine and alcohol and that "the final straw" was that she had approached him sexually. He specified that she had performed fellatio on him the night before. He was directed to call Child Protective Services.

Investigators interviewed Richard and his parents, Roger (48) and Allison (29) 2 days later. Allison admitted that she had been "stoned" for most of a 4-day period ending the night of the alleged offense. Roger had been out of town on business at the time. She remembered being in Richard's room and acknowledged that she "could have done it." She said that she had a "very serious problem" and accepted her husband's demand that she enter a treatment facility immediately. She was admitted to an inpatient chemical dependency program that day.

Descriptive Information

Roger (48) is an insurance and financial planning consultant. His first marriage, to Richards' mother, ended in divorce 5 years ago when she left the state to "marry another man" after "years of arguments and hassles." He married Allison 2 years ago, describing her as a "gorgeous young thing who wanted to be taken care of." He described their marriage as "amicable and pleasant" until she started drinking heavily 6 months ago. He hadn't been aware of her cocaine use until he recently noticed how much money was being spent out of her checking account. He noted that he works long hours and spends quite a bit of time out of town on business.

Allison (29) had not been married before. She had been working as a topless dancer for 2 years before marrying Roger and has not worked out of the home since then. She reported that she married him because he was a "kind man who could give me a way out of that life." She acknowledged a long history of polydrug use before she met Roger, which she had kept hidden from him.

Richard (15) is an only child who is in the 10th grade of a private high school. He has had an excellent behavioral and aca-

demic record and is described as mature and responsible. He reports feeling good about his parents' divorce because of their
arguments but misses seeing his mother. He reports liking Allison
but "not as a mother."

Crisis Intervention

Allison completed a 28-day detoxification and treatment program. She was seen as having both alcohol and cocaine dependence
along with major depression and evidence of eating-disordered
behavior at points of her life. During and after the inpatient treatment, she was also seen by a counselor to focus on sexuality issues.

Allison reported her history, focusing on her physical attractiveness in contrast to a perceived lack of affection and nurturance
for most of her life. She remembered being entered in beauty
contests and modeling from age 6 through adolescence. She also
reported almost constant dieting throughout adolescence. She was
the youngest of three children but always felt that her siblings,
peers, and even parents were "jealous" and she never felt close to
any of them. She sees herself as having been "an obnoxious snob"
during her young adult years. She dated little because "all the boys
were just after sex." She later learned that she could "use sex and
my looks to get what I want." During this same time, however,
she also became depressed and began her polydrug use at age 18.
She then reports a cycle of drug use, short-term relationships,
depression, and employment instability. She became a topless dancer because it was "easy work and great money" but quickly used
the money to develop a strong cocaine addiction, using alcohol as
a way to "mellow" her out. After 6 months, she reported hating
the dancing but felt like she had no alternative. She began to look
for a man with whom she could change her life style and found
Roger, a business associate of her employer. She "straightened up"
to make a positive impression and after 2 or 3 months of dating,
married him. She continued her use of cocaine surreptitiously and
at a low level of dosage and frequency throughout their marriage.
She felt that Roger gave her more caring and nurturing than she
had ever felt and reported feeling "very satisfied" with a warm and
intimate sexual relationship. She increased her use of cocaine as
"part of the nurturing feeling—that I really deserved to feel good"
but acknowledged that it quickly got out of control.

During crisis intervention, after discharge, Allison was seen
in individual counseling, marital dyads, triad apology sessions, and

Cocaine Anonymous. During individual sessions, she accepted responsibility for the pedosexual contact, saying that she did, in fact, remember going into Richard's room "to talk" but after a few minutes pulled back the sheets and began licking and stroking his penis until he told her to stop. She did not remember any feelings at the time, whether he was aroused, or what happened afterwards. She repeated the same details to Roger in a marital session and Richard in a triad apology session, clearly accepting the responsibility for the sexual contact as well as the drug use. Both Roger and Richard expressed their support and committed to treatment.

Roger was seen individually and in the marital dyads. He reported feeling "disgusted and ashamed" about the incident but also concerned about Allison's drug use. After talking with Richard, Roger thought Richard had done the right thing and thought he "was not traumatized" and was continuing to "handle it well." He spoke with considerable pride about his son's achievements and maturity, after which he tearfully expressed shame that he had not taken any action sooner regarding Allison's drug dependence. In marital sessions, he provided support for Allison and acknowledged his share of the responsibility for treating her "as a beautiful possession" rather than a partner.

Richard was seen individually and in the apology sessions. He declined the invitation for group counseling. Richard remembered being "shocked" by the sexual incident and denied arousal at that time or since. He remembered being irritated by Allison's presence in his room and frustrated by her "drinking and drugs which I was trying to keep secret from Dad so his feelings wouldn't get hurt." He was tolerating her that night because she said she wanted to "make friends" and then suddenly pulled back the sheets and said "this will make you feel good" and began licking his penis. He told her to stop and she left the room without saying anything else. He remembered not being able to sleep that night and "checking" on Allison twice to find her passed out on her bed. He expressed anger and resentment over "the way she takes advantage of my Dad" but said that he did not want them to divorce as long as "my Dad wants to stay with her." He reported no trauma or adjustment problems as a result of the contact and indicated his support of Allison "as long as she never does drugs again."

Allison was charged with attempted conduct with a minor (under 18, over 15) and received a plea-bargain sentence of 3 years' probation with mandated treatment for the sexual issues as well as chemical dependency. She was ordered to abstain from all drug use, including alcohol. She was permitted to continue to live in the family home.

Ongoing Treatment

Allison's individual treatment focused on her responsibility for self-control and appropriate expression of needs and feelings. She gained insight into her needs for nurturance and acceptance as a whole person and began setting priorities on ways that she could appropriately take care of herself (especially the "lost child" within her). Individual treatment paralleled her work in the 12-step program of Cocaine Anonymous. She was specifically encouraged to be aware of, and express, her own affective and sexual needs rather than relying on "pleasing behaviors." She reported particular success with an increase in nonsexual touching and stroking, leading to more relaxed sexual contacts and "more orgasms than I've ever had." As confirmed by random testing, she remained drug-free throughout treatment.

Marital sessions focused on these same issues along with a variety of ways that power, communication, and responsibility could be shared more equally. Allison became more involved in Roger's business and learned basic computer skills to assist both in his business and in household financial management. Roger, in turn, reduced his work load and spent more time with Allison on business and family matters. Roger, also, reported a great improvement in their sexual relationship.

Family sessions replaced the individual sessions for Roger and Richard. Expanding on the marital sessions, responsibility and control issues were addressed, with some shifting of tasks and expectations. Allison expressed her desire to be in more of a "mother role" for Richard, and they agreed on some areas where she could provide support without trying to "be friends."

Termination

Allison and the family were successfully terminated from treatment, with the permission of the probation department, after 19 months. Her risk of recidivism regarding the sexual contact was seen as minimal and Richard, now 17, was seen as clearly able to protect himself. Her risk of relapse into the chemical dependency was seen as higher and she was mandated to continue Cocaine Anonymous and random testing for the remainder of her probation. She obtained a part-time job working for the facility where she was treated as an outreach coordinator.

Two years after termination, follow-up indicated that Richard was attending college away from home and that the marital relationship continued "with a few problems." Allison was employed full-time at the treatment facility. She reported remaining drug-free.

Case Study I
C/Adu, I, Unknown—Isolated Treatment of Victim

(Adapted from Rencken, R.H. (in press). Physical and Sexual Abuse: Impact and Intervention. In D. Capuzzi & D. Gross, *Youth at Risk: A Resource for Counselors, Teachers, and Parents.*)

Presenting Problem

Jason is a 9-year-old who was voluntarily turned over to Child Protective Services by his father and stepmother on grounds that he was dangerous to his younger sisters (ages 5 and 2) because of physical attacks, one alleged attempt at setting fire to the 5-year-old's bed, and fondling and attempting oral sex with both younger sisters. The father and stepmother had previously relinquished custody of Jason's 11-year-old sister after she had apparently initiated sexual contact with him, the 5-year-old, and at least two children in a day-care center. The father and stepmother had reluctantly assumed custody of the three oldest children about 18 months previously after the children were removed from the mother's custody in another state. In that investigation it was alleged that the mother had performed mutual oral and manual sex with Jason and his older sister and forced these two children to perform oral sex and coitus with each other in front of a group of adults. She would severely spank Jason (more intensely than the others) and afterwards "make up" for the spanking by performing fellatio on him. The mother was charged with sexual abuse but fled the state to avoid prosecution. The father and stepmother acknowledged increasingly severe physical punishment of Jason but denied sexual abuse (this was corroborated by the children). They refused participation in treatment and eventually permanently relinquished custody of all three oldest children to the state.

Jason was placed in foster care and individual therapy was initiated. He was in five foster placements in 4 months because of his behavior, which included fondling younger children, urinating and defecating in corners, and stealing. Individual therapy included attempts at appropriate expression of feelings (verbal and through art and play), trust building, and limit setting. The individual therapist also provided supportive counseling to the foster parents. Jason was placed in a self-contained emotionally handicapped (EH) class.

Ongoing Treatment

Jason was placed in a foster home after 4 months and remained in that home. Two years after the natural father relinquished custody, the parental rights were severed and he was adopted by the foster parents.

Individual therapy continued to focus on appropriate self-control and dealing with limits, as well as positive expression of feelings and needs. He also was given medication (Imipramine, 25 mg per day), which seemed to have a positive effect on his ability to attend and remain on task. His play in and out of therapy sessions became more focused; for example, he completed jigsaw puzzles for the first time. Although he sometimes expressed "missing" his sisters, he focused more on the foster family and was particularly enthusiastic about family activities. He seemed to remember little about events that happened with his mother, but frequently described his father and stepmother as "mean" because they "hit us all the time." He used the foam bat to hit the adult doll figures that he had labeled as "them." He also built elaborate castles of blocks with the dolls of the foster family inside and "them" outside. Gradually, he began building the castles without "them" and then moved to using the doll house for "family" play. He made great progress in his issues of anxiety/rejection and seemed to bond with the foster parents.

The foster parents were seen regularly and also completed a parenting skills course at the community college. They received support and encouragement along with specific problem-solving techniques. They reported that the aggressive and sexual behavior continued for several months but then subsided, although Jason still tested limits and got into more power struggles than their other (natural) child. They also had consistent problems with lies, although that also decreased in frequency.

Jason remained in the self-contained EH placement for 3 years, with increased mainstreaming during the last year. During this time, he improved from pre-readiness skills to 3rd-grade level achievement (still 3 years behind age peers). His impulse control and attention improved dramatically.

Sexual issues were specifically addressed through the use of age-appropriate sex education media jointly used by counselor and foster parents. He role-played protection skills; the situation was also reversed so he could experience how it "must feel" when he touched other children. Anatomically correct dolls seemed to be helpful in dealing with these issues.

Termination

Individual and family treatment continued for one year after the adoption (3 years after referral), with a focus on communication, control, and self-esteem issues. Behavioral issues remained a concern but the parents seemed to deal with these adequately and appropriately. There were no indications of sexual acting-out. Follow-up one year after termination indicated continued good adjustment and functioning.

CHAPTER 6

THE ROAD AHEAD

Prevention and Education

"All right," you say, "let's get to the roots of this problem. Let's stop this Band-Aid approach and deal with prevention."

"Where do we start?"

"Why, we start with the children, of course. We teach the children that sexual touching is bad, you can't trust adults even within your own family, and it's their responsibility to "just say no."

"Wait a minute. I thought we were supposed to teach kids that their sexuality is good, that trust is essential, and that abuse is the adult's responsibility."

"Well, that's true too. We'll teach them that good touching like hugs is OK unless they're too close and kissing is OK unless it's too long and washing is OK unless it's in the private parts. But we can't talk about sex because of district policy so we'll tell them not to trust anyone they don't feel comfortable with and we'll tell them that if they report a bad touch from their father, he'll go to prison for a long, long time and then they won't have any more scary feelings."

I hope my colleagues who are involved in prevention programs will forgive me. I truly do empathize with the task of translating this incredibly complex problem into programs that are helpful, understandable, and accurate for children, adolescents, and adults. We question our success in prevention programs for substance abusers and dropouts (which are far more tangible and less complex), yet we expect to put together a successful prevention program targeted for the victims rather than the perpetrators of a behavior.

We will focus our attention on prevention programs within school systems although some other programs (church and youth groups) are being put into effect using similar approaches. We will then look at broader educational programs and related societal issues.

School prevention programs typically focus on identification of abuse (signs, symptoms, and reporting), body ownership, trust issues, and saying no (the latter three sometimes grouped under "empowerment") (Tennant, 1988; Tharinger, Krivacska, Laye-McDonough, Jamison, Vincent, & Hedlund, 1988). Curricula that are aimed at children frequently use books in conjunction with movies, puppet play, drawing/coloring pages, or behavioral role-playing. Typical messages include:

- the right to safety of the child's own body and nobody else's right to touch it;
- saying no to unwanted or uncomfortable touches;
- assertiveness;
- good versus bad secrets; and
- reporting abuse.

Handled correctly, these messages make sense. We certainly want our children to have the ability to protect themselves, or at least provide a layer of protection. Having our children memorize a phone number helps but it doesn't alleviate our responsibility to see that they don't get lost.

Tharinger et al. (1988) reviewed prevention programs with some cogent observations. I would summarize two empirical and two philosophical concerns that they raised.

The first empirical concern is whether children, particularly young children, understand the messages that are intended for them. The confusion that was described at the beginning of this section is probably magnified in the mind of a young child without the developmental ability to abstract, generalize, and apply the information. One example, from my experience, is that children will not be able to explain what "private parts" are or else they will repeat a definition given to them like "parts covered by a bathing suit" without any idea that these adults are talking about their "pee-pee." Likewise, although "good touch-bad touch" concepts seem to make sense to us as adults, children have difficulty conceptualizing discomfort and questionable touches—in their mind, bad touch hurts but we know that most pedosexual contact does not, in fact, physically hurt. Many children, despite our hard efforts, simply "don't get it" and there is essentially no empirical evidence that they do understand.

The second empirical criticism is that there is little or no evidence that even if children "get it," there will be any lasting effect. The layer of protection may be too thin against the other complex and powerful variables that create sexual abuse. It is almost impossible to point to any reduction in sexual abuse as the result of school prevention programs. (There are, of course, some logical research problems in trying to prove the negative.) There may be an increase in reporting of abuse after some programs that focus on that aspect *and* provide the mechanisms for reports. Do prevention programs prevent? The case is yet to be proven.

With my training in sexology as well as counseling, I was delighted that Tharinger et al. (1988) asked the philosophical question, "How can we teach about sexual abuse without dealing with sex?" With the continuing, and perhaps even growing, resistance to sex education, many programs have to emphasize safety instead of sex and use euphemisms (private parts) or indirect references. It's like discussing "quacking" without being able to talk about ducks. The programs may even add to sex-negativity because "bad touch" and "say no" certainly receive more emphasis than "sex is a wonderful thing between consenting adults." If sex-negativity has to be mentioned, it should be balanced by developmentally appropriate sex-positive messages.

The other major philosophical question is whether the potential (or actual) victims should bear the responsibility for solving this problem. Some critics point out the unfairness, ineffectiveness, and negative effects of placing that burden (Crewdson, 1988; Conte, Rosen, & Saperstein, 1986; Krazier, 1986) and suggest that this may take the focus off the true societal and individual causes of pedosexual behavior.

Although school-based prevention programs may be necessary, their effectiveness is, at best, limited. Has the school lunch program solved the hunger problem in America? No. Why? Because despite the help, it does not deal with the bigger economic, employment, and societal issues. And, besides, the kids don't eat the lunches!

The need for more general education is clear. That's what this book is all about. The professions directly involved with the problem as well as the general public need to understand, in at least a basic way, that this is a problem rooted in many societal issues that we have chosen to ignore, resist, or deny.

We can educate toward the concept of sex positivism, the notion that sexuality is a positive, vital force within each of us—a force of caring, love and concern, a force of intimacy and vulnerability, a force of pleasure, awareness, and spirituality. Sex becomes negative only when we let it.

We can educate toward the concept of gender equity. Russell (1986) effectively articulated that two of the most neglected causes of incest, rape, extrafamilial sexual abuse, and sexual harassment are "the way males are socialized to behave sexually and the power structure within which they act out this sexuality." Sexual abuse cannot exist in a society of sexual equality. Almost by definition, it is an offense of the stronger (usually men) against the weak, created out of a lack of true personal power and self-control. Gender equity must not only be pursued at the societal level by truly addressing issues of equal opportunity and rights, but it also must be pursued in the next generation, teaching children that they are valued equally, treated equitably, and encouraged enthusiastically, regardless of their sex. Children must feel that they can line up together; learn about reading, math, and sexuality together; and play together. This should be a basic assumption rather than a constant struggle. This is *real* empowerment.

We can educate toward the concept of sexual literacy. As a society, we can acknowledge that children and adults need and are entitled to accurate, developmentally appropriate, and nonjudgmental information about sexuality, intimacy, and relationships.

We can educate toward the concept of positive self-esteem. When each of us feels good about ourselves—our body, our feelings, our successes and failures—the need for controlling and exploiting others simply does not exist.

We can educate toward the concept of healthy family functioning. The basic foundation of our society need not be left to chance. We can learn how to be more responsible, effective, and sharing family members.

The Challenge

Sexual abuse (and the concept of pedosexual behavior) is one of the most complex problems that counselors and other helping professionals will face in their careers. The issues are societal and, yet, dramatically affect the lives of individuals. We are faced, as we have been before, with healing the effects of sexism, family dysfunction, exploitation of power, sexual ignorance, and our continuing failure to protect and support our children.

It is heartening that in many cases with offenders, and in most cases with victims and survivors, we *can immeasurably* help the healing process. The word "immeasurably" is used with two meanings—we know as we see families reunited or children functioning well that we have done a great job, but the results are difficult to measure and quantify. This difficulty in substantiation is critical within the political arena when we try to make a case for treatment rather than warehousing in prison. It also damages our credibility within the criminal justice system.

Research, then, becomes a vital need, but research design seems impossible. How do we control the innumerable variables? What is our consensus regarding treatment goals? What exactly is "good versus bad touch"? What is the true repeat offense rate? By whom? Against whom? Is there a uniform notion of severity? How accurate are our arousal measures?

We, as counselors, are in an almost untenable position, but we will continue to face the challenge. The counselor working with pedosexual behavior may need more and better skills than most others. This work demands expertise in individual counseling with men, women, and children; group approaches; dealing with the criminal justice and child protection systems; marital and family therapy; sex education and therapy; substance abuse; and the ability to work in integrated treatment teams over the long range.

How can we plan for the future? We have to recognize that our tremendous effort is barely scratching the surface. Remember the early metaphor of the snow-covered volcano? We are handling the volcano with snow shovels. There are more of us involved in the struggle and we know more about what we're doing, so that we can identify the crevices and the obstacles and maybe even escape more consistently from the lava flow, but we can neither stop it nor accurately predict it. We will have to face the challenge for precisely as long as society tolerates the problems noted above.

How can we keep going? How can we continue to face the challenge? The answer is easy and, yet, frustrating. We get our reward and encouragement from the teary-eyed offender hugging his daughter for the first time in a year; from the confident smile of a mother at reunification; from the pride of a young survivor graduating from high school; and from the almost embarrassing elation of an adult survivor reporting her first orgasm.

The challenge is for everyone to face, like it or not. Some of us can and will do more than others in directly tackling the tasks, but the challenge is clearly societal and professional.

The challenge is ours. For the children!

GLOSSARY

Anilingus—Oral stimulation of the anal area.

Child Protective Service(s)—Division of county or state government responsible for child welfare. Usually the primary agency for reporting any child abuse or neglect.

Coitus—Genital intercourse; penetration of penis into vagina.

Cunnilingus—Oral (literally, tongue) stimulation of the female genital area.

Deviate/deviant behavior—Behavior that is different from the statistical (or societal) norm. Criteria are usually relativistic and nonscientific. Frequently used in a perjorative manner. See also "Paraphilia."

Digital penetration—Insertion of the finger(s) into the anus or vagina.

Dyad (triad) therapy—Conjoint therapy with two (three) people. Sometimes used as a "bridge" from individual to family therapy.

Ejaculation—Flow or spurting of semen from the penis. Differentiating it from urination may be important evidence in investigation.

Ephebophilia—Compulsive attraction to male adolescents.

Exploitation—Sexual abuse of children that may not involve physical contact; for example, nude or sexually explicit photography. In some jurisdictions it is a criminal offense separate from sexual abuse or molestation.

Fellatio—Oral stimulation of the penis.

Fondling—In general use, touching affectionately. In sexual offense, touching or stroking breast, genital, anal, or buttock areas.

Genital apposition—Rubbing genitals together without penetration, either while clothed or not. A frequently reported behavior that may not be illegal in some jurisdictions.

Hebephilia—Compulsive attraction to female adolescents.

Homosexuality—Sexual behavior or orientation directed toward the same sex. Same-sex behavior in pedosexual contact may not be indicative of true homosexual preference in either partner.

171

Male victims frequently have concerns about their orientation. Homophobia, the fear of homosexuality, is frequently present in offenders, victims, and adult survivors.

Hymen—Membrane that may wholly or partially cover the vaginal opening. Its absence does not necessarily indicate sexual penetration, although certain patterns of tearing may be used as evidence of penetration if appropriately documented in a medical examination.

Incest—Nonspousal sexual contact within the nuclear family. Definitions vary from one jurisdiction to another and from one researcher to another, making the term ambiguous. Recently, it has more accurately been replaced by the term "intrafamilial sexual abuse." Although sibling contact is incestuous, it may or may not be abusive and is generally excluded.

Intercourse—Contact involving the genitals of at least one person. Although frequently used synonymously with coitus, it is a more general term that may not be accurately descriptive. Legally, defined differently by various jurisdictions to possibly include coitus, oral contact, anal penetration, digital penetration, or penile-femoral contact.

Intergenerational boundary—The theoretical boundary that exists between adults and children within a family.

Intrafamilial sexual abuse (contact)—Sexual contact within the family or family living unit as opposed to extrafamilial contact.

Labia—The lips or rolls of tissue external to the vaginal opening.

Mandatory reporting—The law, in all states, requiring the reporting of any child abuse. Jurisdictions vary as to whether knowledge has to be direct (from the child) or whether suspicion of abuse has to be reported. The "good faith" reporter is generally protected from liability.

Mandatory sentencing—The law, in some jurisdictions, requiring a specific minimal sentence for a crime without judicial discretion. In Arizona, for example, first-time sexual abuse offenders are required to spend a minimum of 12 years in prison with no probation available. If convicted on two counts, the minimum is 42 years. Preliminary reports are that this has reduced convictions and, certainly, reduced treatment options.

Masturbation—Sexual manual self-stimulation. Although also often used to mean genital stroking of another person, as in "mutual masturbation," this seems less clear than a more behavioral description such as "genital stroking/rubbing" or "manual clitoral stimulation."

Molestation—Any sexually abusive contact between an adult and child. Not useful because of its vague and judgmental usage.

Paraphilia—The diagnostic classification for behaviors or arousal patterns that deviate from the norm. Pedophilia is included in this classification. Researchers are still struggling with the classification and nomenclature of the paraphilias. Paraphilias may or may not have legal sanctions.

Parole—Postimprisonment supervision. Jurisdictions vary on the length of parole and extent of supervision.

Pederasty—Classically, mens' love of boys, with or without sexual behavior. It has also come to be used for man-to-boy sex, particularly anal contact, making the term vague and not helpful. May still be considered a criminal offense in some jurisdictions.

Pedophilia—Although changed somewhat from the DSM-III to the DSM-IIIR, it still generally refers to a consistent sexual preference for, or arousal pattern to, prepubertal children. It is generally compulsive and frequently exclusive, with multiple or even high-frequency behaviors.

Pedosexual—Used by this author to describe any sexual contact involving a child without judgment or diagnostic/prognostic implications.

Penetration—Insertion of finger, penis, or object into the anus, vagina, or mouth.

Penile transducer—(Also known as plethysmograph)—instrument used to measure penile erection/arousal for either diagnostic or treatment monitoring purposes.

Plea bargain—Agreement between the defense and prosecution where the defendant pleads guilty (or no contest) to one or more charges in return for dismissal or reduction of other charges. Also referred to as "copping" (change of plea).

Pornography—Media, typically sexually explicit, that are judged by society to be unacceptable. The term is virtually meaningless and vague. Behavioral descriptors seem more helpful; for example, nudity, sexual explicitness, simulated rape, and so forth. Children may become objects of media known collectively as "kiddie porn," whose consumers are likely to be pedophiles. Distinctions between "hard-core" and "soft-core" or between "erotica" and "exploitation" have not been helpful.

Probation—Supervised alternative to prison with varying conditions and restrictions. Typically, violation of probation results in a revocation process and possible incarceration.

Rape—Coitus (or in some jurisdictions, any sexual penetration or attempted penetration) with an unwilling partner, typically involving force or physical violence.

Rebonding—The process of rebuilding the affectional/nurturance bond between parent (usually mother) and child.

Sexual abuse—Sexual contact between an adult and child with damaging or potentially damaging consequences. In some jurisdictions, may also apply to adult-adult contact that does not meet other criteria of sexual assault or rape.

Sexual addiction—Sexually compulsive (nonspecific) behavior that produces an addictive drive for sexual activity. The behavior may be consensual adult activity, multiple or serial partners, masturbation, exhibitionism, voyeurism, and so forth, frequently in combination. Children may be objects for an outlet for the sexual addict.

Sexually transmitted disease (STD)—Any disease that can be transmitted through sexual contact. Includes the traditional "venereal diseases" such as gonorrhea, syphilis, chancroid, and also AIDS. Children are, of course, at risk of contracting these, and an STD screen will normally be done as part of an initial medical evaluation.

"Skin-to-skin" contact—Terminology used by law enforcement or prosecutors to indicate touch or other contact without clothing as a barrier.

Taboo, incest—The essentially universal cultural proscription against adult-child sexual contact within the family.

Vagina—The birth canal. The space/sheath (or more accurately, potential space) to contain the penis. Frequently misused to refer to the external genitalia (labia or vulva).

Vulva—Generic term for the external female genitalia.

Work furlough/release—A program that allows a convicted offender time to work at a regular job and serve "jail time" in the evenings or weekends.

RESOURCES

Adults Molested as Children United, c/o Institute for the Community As Extended Family, P.O. Box 952, San Jose, CA 95108; (408) 280-5055
  Groups for survivors; nationwide referrals to local groups.
Child Help National Child Abuse Hotline, P.O. Box 630, Hollywood, CA 90028; 1-800-422-4453
  Survivors of childhood abuse program provides crisis counseling and information on location of nationwide services for adults molested as children; publishes *Survivor's Guide.*
Incest Recovery Association, 6200 North Central Expressway, Suite 209, Dallas, TX 75206; (214) 373-6607
  Provides therapy groups for male and female survivors of incest; provides public and professional education programs; distributes educational material and a newsletter.
Incest Survivor Information Exchange (I.S.I.E.), P.O. Box 3399, New Haven, CT 06515; (203) 389-5166
  Provides newsletter as a forum for female and male survivors of incest to publish their thoughts, writings, art work, and to exchange information.
Incest Survivors Resource Network International (ISRNI), P.O. Box 911, Hicksville, NY 11802; (516) 935-3031
  Provides educational resources through participation in national and international committees and conferences.
National Organization for Victim Assistance (NOVA), 717 D Street, NW, Suite 200, Washington, DC 20004; (202) 393-NOVA
  24-hour-a-day service for information about local victim assistance groups.
Survivors Newsletter Collective, c/o Women's Center, 46 Pleasant Street, Cambridge, MA 02139
  A volunteer collective of adult women survivors of childhood sexual abuse; publishes quarterly newsletter *For Crying Out Loud.*

Survivors of Incest Anonymous (SIA), P.O. Box 21817, Baltimore, MD 21222-6817; (301) 282-3400

Provides self-help groups for survivors of incest based on a 12-step program for women and men 18 years and older.

Voices in Action, Inc., P.O. Box 148309, Chicago, IL 60614; (312) 327-1500

Provides national network of incest survivors and supporters of survivors; referral service; survival packet of resource material; newsletter, and national conference.

Note: From *Adults Molested as Children: A Survivor's Manual for Women and Men* (p. 61) by E. Bear, 1988, Orwell, VT: Safer Society Press.

REFERENCES

Abel, G., & Becker, J. (1984). *The treatment of child molesters.* New York: Columbia University Press.

Alexander, P.C., & Lupfer, S.L. (1987). Family characteristics and long-term consequences associated with sexual abuse. *Archives of Sexual Behavior, 16,* 235–245.

American Psychiatric Association. (1987). *Diagnostic and statistical manual of mental disorders, Third edition, Revised.* Washington, DC: Author.

Barbach, L. (1975). *For yourself.* Garden City, NY: Anchor Press.

Barbach, L. (1982). *For each other.* New York: Anchor Press.

Bass, E., & Davis, L. (1988). *The courage to heal.* New York: Harper & Row.

Bass, E., & Thornton, L. (1983). *I never told anyone.* New York: Harper & Row.

Bear, E. (1988). *Adults molested as children: A survivor's manual for women and men.* Orwell, VT: Safer Society Press.

Bell, A., & Weinberg, M. (1978). *Homosexualities.* New York: Simon & Schuster.

Brady, K. (1979). *Father's days: A true story.* New York: Dell.

Carnes, P.J. (1983). *The sexual addiction.* Minneapolis: Comp Care.

Conte, J.R., Rosen, C., & Saperstein, L. (1986). An analysis of programs to prevent the sexual victimization of children. *Journal of Primary Prevention, 6,* 141–155.

Crewdson, J. (1988). *By silence betrayed: Sexual abuse of children in America.* Boston: Little, Brown.

Damon, L., & Waterman, J. (1986). Parallel group treatment of children and their mothers. In K. MacFarlane and J. Waterman (Eds.), *Sexual abuse of young children* (pp. 244–298). New York: Guilford.

Dobson, J. (1970). *Dare to discipline.* Wheaton, IL: Tyndale.

Elkind, D. (1967). Egocentrism in adolescence. *Child Development, 38,* 1025–1035.

Erikson, E. (1968). *Identity: Youth and crisis.* New York: Norton.

Finkelhor, D. (1979). *Sexually victimized children*. New York: Free Press.

Finkelhor, D. (1984). *Child sexual abuse*. New York: Free Press.

Fraser, S. (1988). *My father's house*. New York: Ticknor & Fields.

Friedman, S. (1988). A family systems approach to treatment. In L.E. Walker, *Handbook on sexual abuse of children* (pp. 326–349). New York: Springer.

Gardner, R.A. (1987). *The parental alienation syndrome and the differentiation between fabricated and genuine child sex abuse*. Cresskill, NJ: Creative Therapeutic.

Giaretto, H. (1982). *Integrated treatment of child sexual abuse*. Palo Alto, CA: Science & Behavior Books.

Groth, A.N. (1979). *Men who rape: The psychology of the offender*. New York: Plenum Press.

Groth, A.N., & Birnbaum, H.J. (1978). Adult sexual orientation and attraction to underage persons. *Archives of Sexual Behavior, 7*, 175–181.

Herman, J. (1981). *Father/daughter incest*. Cambridge, MA: Harvard University Press.

Johanek, M.F. (1988). Treatment of male victims of child sexual abuse in military service. In S.M. Sgroi (Ed.), *Vulnerable populations, Vol. 1* (pp. 103–114). Lexington, MA: Lexington Books.

Kosky, R. (1983). Child suicidal behavior. *Journal of Child Psychology and Psychiatry and Allied Disciplines, 24*, 457–468.

Krazier, S.K. (1986). Rethinking prevention. *Child Abuse and Neglect, 10*, 259–261.

Levin, S.M., & Stava, L. (1987). Personality characteristics of sex offenders: A review. *Archives of Sexual Behavior, 16*, 57–79.

Lew, M. (1988). *Victims no longer: Men recovering from incest*. New York: Ruby Street Press.

Long, S. (1986). Guidelines for treating young children. In K. MacFarlane & J. Waterman, *Sexual abuse of young children* (pp. 220–243). New York: Guilford.

MacFarlane, K. (1986). Child sexual abuse allegations in divorce proceedings. In K. MacFarlane & J. Waterman, *Sexual abuse of young children* (pp. 121–150). New York: Guilford.

MacFarlane, K., & Waterman, J. (1986). *Sexual abuse of young children*. New York: Guilford.

Maurer, A. (Ed.) (1972–1988). *The last report*. Newsletter of the Committee to End Violence Against the Next Generation, Berkeley, CA.

McGovern, K., & Peters, J. (1988). Guidelines for assessing sex offenders. In L.E. Walker, *Handbook on sexual abuse of children* (pp. 350–370). New York: Springer.

McKenry, P.C., Fishler, C.L., & Kelly, C. (1982). Adolescent suicide. *Clinical Pediatrics, 21*, 266–270.

McNaron, T.A., & Morgan, Y. (1982). *Voices in the night.* Pittsburgh: Cleis Press.

Morris, M. (1982). *If I should die before I wake.* New York: Dell.

Oaklander, V. (1978). *Windows to our children.* Moab, UT: Real People Press.

Porter, F.S., Blick, L.C., & Sgroi, S.M. (1982). Treatment of the sexually abused child. In S.M. Sgroi, *Handbook of clinical intervention in child sexual abuse* (pp. 115–130). Lexington, MA: Lexington Books.

Rencken, R.H. (1986). Sex positivism for mental health counselors. In A.J. Palmo & W.J. Weikel (Eds.), *Foundations of mental health counseling* (pp. 91–94). Springfield, IL: Charles C Thomas.

Rush, F. (1980). *The best kept secret.* Englewood Cliffs, NJ: Prentice-Hall.

Russell, D.E. (1986). *The secret trauma.* New York: Basic Books.

Salkind, N.J., & Ambron, S.R. (1987). *Child development* (5th ed). New York: Holt, Rinehart & Winston.

Spiegel, L.D. (1988). Child abuse hysteria and the elementary school counselor. *Elementary School Guidance and Counseling, 22*, 275–283.

Tennant, C.G. (1988). Preventive sexual abuse programs: Problems and possibilities. *Elementary School Guidance and Counseling, 23*, 48–53.

Tharinger, D.J., Krivacska, J.J., Laye-McDonough, M., Jamison, L., Vincent, G.G., & Hedlund, A.D. (1988). Prevention of child sexual abuse: An analysis of issues, educational programs, and research findings. *School Psychology Review, 17*, 614–634.

Waterman, J. (1986). Developmental considerations. In K. MacFarlane & J. Waterman (Eds.), *Sexual abuse of young children* (pp. 15–29). New York: Guilford.

Waterman, J., & Lusk, R. (1986). Scope of the problem. In K. MacFarlane & J. Waterman (Eds.)., *Sexual abuse of young children* (pp. 3–14). New York: Guilford.

Wolf, S.C., Conte, J.R., & Engel-Meinig, K. (1988). Assessment and treatment of sex offenders in a community setting. In L.E. Walker, *Handbook for sexual abuse of children* (pp. 371–390). New York: Springer.

Yates, A. (1978). *Sex without shame.* New York: Morrow.

Zilbergeld, B. (1978). *Male sexuality.* New York: Bantam Books.

INDEX

Addicted/compulsive offender
  behavior pattern, 94–95
  treatment strategies, 107–108
Adolescent/adult age combination,
  case studies, 143–147, 151–
  153, 157–161
Adolescent survivor
  case study, 151–153
  intervention strategies, 61–81
  resistance to treatment, 63
  runaway behavior, 63–64
  victim/survivor role confusion,
  61–64
Adult survivor
  case study, 154–156
  interventions, 119–125
Advocacy. See Intervention
Affective awareness
  offender, 88, 98, 105
  in young child, 36
Age combinations. See also specific
  combinations
  adolescent/adolescent, 8
  adolescent/adult, 9
  child/adolescent, 8
  child/adult, 9
  child/child, 8
Anger and hostility. See also Rage
  in mother, 113
  repressed
    in adolescent, 71
    in middle child, 46
Apology sessions
  with adolescent, 72
  with middle child, 48–51
  offender, 101–102
Assessment process with offender
  cautions regarding, 90–91
  goals, 86

  techniques, 87–89
  for treatment planning, 86–87
  types of, 85–86
Attachment to counselor, young
  child, 35–36
Attitudes and beliefs of counselors,
  12

Body image, in adolescent, 75

Career issues, offender, 106
Case studies
  adolescent/adult, 143–147,
    151–153, 157–161
  Allison, age 29, 157–161
  child/adult, 127–143, 147–156,
    161–163
  Cindy, age 16, 151–153
  Debra, age 26, 154–156
  Frank, age 52, 150–151
  Jason, age 9, 161–163
  Joan, age 16, 127–136
  Kevin, age 9, 136–143
  Marianne, age 17, 143–147
  Norman, age 26, 147–150
Categorization. See Taxonomy
Child
  middle (7 to puberty)
    indicators of abuse, 41
    intervention strategies, 39–61
  as primary client, 14
  young (under 7)
    family sessions and, 117–118
    intervention strategies, 30–39
Child/adult age combination, case
  studies, 127–143, 147–156,
  161–163

181

Child Protective Services
    intervention role, 25–26
    investigative role, 25, 42–43
    teamwork with, 65
    treatment planning role, 95
Civil court, 24–25
Classification of pedosexual
    behavior. *See* Taxonomy
Clinical interview, with offender,
    87–88
Coercion issue, youthful offenders,
    79
Communication skills, offender, 98
Confidentiality issue, 64, 67, 84
Control issues, offender, 98, 106
Counselor
    attachment of young child to,
        35–36
    attitudes, values, and beliefs, 12
    behavior with young child, 34
    child's perception of role, 67
    court appearance settings, 24
    "offender-bashing," 66
    philosophical assumptions,
        13–16
    roles in legal system, 23
    support role with adolescent,
        66
    support role with middle child,
        41–43
Court system, 24–25
Criminal court, 24
Criminal justice system, 22–27
Crisis intervention
    adolescent, 65–70
    delayed, 64–65, 68–70
    middle child, 44–45
    offender, 99–101

"Damaged goods" syndrome, 34, 45
    in adolescent, 70
Delayed crisis intervention, 64–65,
    68–70
Depression
    in adolescent, 70
    in middle child, 46
    in mother, 113
    in young child, 35
Developmental history of offender,
    88

Developmental issues
    adolescent, 62–64
    middle child, 40
Diagnosis, DSM-III and DSM-IIIR,
    91–92
Divorce court, 24
Dynamics. *See also* Offender
    dynamics
    family, 19–21
    individual, 21–22
    individual offenders, 104
    societal, 17–18
    systems, 104

Eating disorders, adolescents, 64
Education, 165–169
Educational groups, in treatment of
    offender, 96
Empowerment
    adolescent, 74–76
    adult survivors, 123
    middle child, 52–55
    offender, 105–106
    young child, 37–38
Environment for treatment, young
    child, 33–34
Ephebophilia, 77
Exploratory behavior. *See* Sexually
    related behavior
Extrafamilial setting
    case studies, 147–151, 154–156
    middle child victims, 57–61

Family
    apology sessions, 101–102
    characteristics, 115
    intervention strategies, 111–
        119
    reunification, 119
    treatment goals, 114
    as victims, 112–114
    visitation, 118–119
Family court, 24
Family drawings, 52
Family dynamics, 19–21
Family system
    father-child dyad, 117
    husband-wife dyad, 116
    mother-child dyad, 116
    mother-father-child triad, 117

Family systems strategy, 111
Family techniques, for treatment of
    youthful offender, 80–81
Family therapy, in treatment of
    offender, 96
Father/offender, relationship with
    middle child, 54
Fathers
    dependent, case study, 136–
      143
    dictatorial/possessive, 19
    case study, 127–136
    immature/irresponsible, 19
Fear behavior
    in adolescent, 68, 70
    middle child, 44, 46
    young child, 30, 35
Female offender, 108
    case study, 157–161
    and middle child, 60
Female survivor, 120–124

Gender equity education, 168
Grief, adult survivors, 123
Group therapy
    with adolescent, 73
    in treatment of offender, 96
Guilt factor
    in adolescent, 70
    adult survivors, 122
    middle child, 44, 45–46
    mother, 113
    in young child, 34

Hebephilia, 77
Homophobic concerns, counselor
    discussion, 61
Homophobic concerns, male
    survivor, 124
Hostility. *See* Anger and hostility
"Humping," in young child, 31

Impact
    on counseling profession, 6
    on families, victims, and
      survivors, 4–6
    measurement, 4
    on society, 6

Incarceration in treatment of
    offender, 97
Incidence research, statistics, 3–4
Individual therapy, in treatment of
    offender, 96
Infantile regression, 36
Integrated treatment of offender,
    84–85
Interpersonal relationships,
    offender, 98–99
Intervention process, 25–27
Intervention strategies
    adolescents, 61–81
    adult survivors, 119–125
    family, 111–119
    middle child (7 to puberty),
      39–61
    offender, 83–109
    victim, 29–81
    young child (under 7), 30–39
Interviews. *See* Clinical interview
Intimacy patterns
    adolescent survivors, 63
    offender, 105
Intrafamilial setting, case studies,
    127–147, 151–153, 157–163
Isolated treatment of offender,
    84–85
Isolated treatment of victim, case
    study, 161–163

Jigsaw puzzle metaphor, 17,
    102–105, 115
Juvenile court, 24

Language. *See* Sexual language use
Legal issues, 22–27

Male survivor, 124–125
Male victim
    adolescent, 78
    middle child, 60–61
    young, 38–39
Manipulative behavior, offender, 91
Mother
    loyalty to spouse vs. protection
      of child, 112
    play group participation, 37

protection of middle child, 53–54

rage toward, 66

rebonding with, 75

trust-building role in treatment, 32–33

Nightmares, in young child, 30

Offender
accountability to society, 15
arousal patterns, 104
disinhibiting factors, 102–103
family of origin, 103
intervention strategies, 83–109
pattern analysis, 102–105
recidivism, 13–14
regressed, 83–107
responsibility for abuse, 15
sex history, 103–104
youthful, 79–81
Offender dynamics
addicted/compulsive offender, 10
individuals, 21–22
pedophile, 9–10
rapist, 10–11
regressed offender, 9
symptomatic, 11

Pattern analysis, in treatment of offender, 102–105
Pedophile
behavior pattern, 93
case studies, 147–151, 154–156
middle child victims, 58
treatment strategies, 107
Pedophilia, 77
Peer relationships
adolescents, 64
middle child, 48
Philosophical assumptions for counselor, 13–16
Physical environment for treatment, 33–34
Physical evidence of abuse, in middle child, 40
Play groups, in treatment of young child, 37

Play therapy, middle child, 51–52
Plethysmograph, 89
Polygraph, 89
Positive attitude on sexuality, 16, 55
Positive regard for client, 16
Power, sense of. See Empowerment
Power relationship, offender, 97–98
Prevention programs in school systems, 165–168
Probation, 96–97, 107
Protection of victim
child protective service role, 25–26, 42
not counselor's role, 42
Pseudoadult child
case study, 143–147
in family dynamics, 20
Pseudomaturity
in adolescent, 71
in middle child, 47
in young child, 35
Psychometric evaluation of offender, 88–89
Psychopharmacological approaches in treatment of offender, 96
Psychophysiological measures, 89

Rage. See also Anger and hostility
male survivor, 124
middle child, 44, 57
toward mother, 66
Rape
victim-blaming syndrome, 77
victim traumatization, 58–59, 77
Rapist
behavior pattern, 95
case study, 151–153
treatment strategies, 107
Rebonding with mother, 75
Regressed offender
behavior pattern, 93
case studies, 127–147, 151–153
treatment strategies, 83–107
Repeated offense risk, 106–107
Report to authorities
adolescent cases, 64–65
confidentiality concerns, 64
middle child cases, 40–43
necessity of, 42
young child cases, 31–32

Research
    design challenge, 169
    obstacles to, 3
Responsibility issue, 15
    and adult survivors, 122
    offender, 90–91, 97, 100–101
    and prevention programs, 167
    youthful offender, 80
Role clarification
    adolescent, 73–74
    middle child, 51–52
Role confusion and blurred role
        boundaries
    in adolescent, 71
    in middle child, 47
    in young child, 35
Runaway behavior, 63–64, 65, 67

"The secret," keeping
    adolescent victim/survivor, 65,
        69
    middle child, 41
Self-esteem
    low
        in adolescent, 70–71
        in middle child, 46
        in young child, 35
        youthful offender, 80
    positive, as educational goal,
        168
Self-help, in treatment of offender,
        96
Self-mastery and control
    in adolescent, 71
    in middle child, 47–48
    in young child, 35
Setting, extrafamilial vs.
        intrafamilial, 7–8
Sex history of offender, 88, 103–
        104
Sex positivism, 168
Sex therapy, marital dyad, 116
Sexual addiction/compulsion, victim
        support, 59
Sexual behavior
    in adolescent, 62–63, 75
    in adult survivor, 123–124
    in middle child victim, 41
Sexual disorders, in offender, 92
Sexual knowledge, adult-type, in
        young child, 30–31

Sexual language use
    in middle child, 41
    in young child, 31
Sexual literacy, as educational goal,
        168
Siblings
    blaming the victim, 113–114
    loyalty to father, 113
    as victim, 113–114
Snow-covered volcano metaphor, 2,
        83, 169
Social skills, poor
    in adolescent, 70–71
    middle child, 46
    young child, 35
Societal dynamics, 17–19
Societal prejudice against offenders,
        12–13
Statistics on sexual abuse, 3–4
Statute of limitations, 65
Substance use/abuse, offender, 92,
        105
Suicide risk
    adolescents, 63, 65, 67
    male survivor, 124
    middle child, 44, 56–57
    offender, 99
    spouse, 99
    victim, 99
Support groups
    adult survivor, 122, 125
    male survivor, 124
Support of victim, counselor's role,
        41–43
Supportive confrontation with
        offender, 100
Symptomatic offender
    and adolescents, 78
    behavior pattern, 95
    case study, 157–161
    treatment strategies, 108
    victim support, 60

Taxonomy, 6–11, 92–95
    age combinations, 7–9
    offender dynamics, 9–11
    setting, 7
    use of, 11
Team treatment, 15
Termination of treatment
    adolescent, 76

middle child, 55–56
offender, 106–107
young child, 38
Terminology
    glossary, 171–175
    taxonomy, 6–11
Treatability of pedosexual
    offenders, 13–14
Treatment as prevention, 14
Treatment of adolescent
    contract, 67
    issues, 70–71
    strategies, 71–76
    termination, 76
Treatment of adult survivor
    counselors, 120
    female, 120–124
    feminist perspective, 120
    male, 124–125
    support groups, 122, 125
Treatment of family
    goals, 114
    interventions, 115–118
Treatment of offender
    goals, 97–99
    limitations on confidentiality,
        84
    long-term vs. short-term, 85
    planning, 95–99
    termination, 106–107
    warnings and cautions, 109
Treatment of young child
    duration, 34

early phase, 32–33
issues, 34–37
therapeutic atmosphere, 33–34
Trust issues
    in adolescent, 65–67, 69, 71
    in middle child, 46–47
    in treatment of offender, 84
    in young child, 35

Validation, sense of, 64–65
Values of counselors, 12
Victim as offender, 79–80
Victim veracity issue
    adolescent, 68
    middle child, 43
Victim vs. survivor, role transition,
    62
Victims
    family members as, 112–114
    intervention strategies, 29–81
    joint victimization by
        pedophiles, 58
    siblings as, 113–114
    unique behaviors, 40–41
Visitation by father, 118–119

Warning signs
    during treatment of adolescent,
        76
    during treatment of middle
        child, 56–57
Withdrawal, in young child, 30